THE MAKING OF A JOURNALIST

"I was happy to read of your fertile period with raptors, DDT, and bird conservation—when you accessed top-notch publication sites and your work was celebrated. I was there. It was a good, important time for all of us! We caught the post-Rachel Carson wave and documented in detail phenomena that she could only sketch out or hypothesize about. David, in my experience you have been an endlessly curious and incisive reporter of science and society."

—*Paul Spitzer, Ph.D., ecologist*

THE MAKING OF A JOURNALIST

Santhi & I: A Memoir

David Radoff Zimmerman

FCP

Full Court Press
Englewood Cliffs, New Jersey

First Edition

Copyright © 2020 by David Radoff Zimmerman

Published in the United States of America by Full Court Press, 601 Palisade Avenue, Englewood Cliffs, NJ 07632 *fullcourtpress.com*

ISBN 978-1-946989-72-7
Library of Congress Control Number: 2020912206

Editing and book design by Barry Sheinkopf

Author photo by Henry Grossman

The author expresses heartfelt thanks to thanks to Bobbie Bristol, Paul Spitzer, Tom Watkins, Dori Gerber, Cindy Eli, J.B. Zimmerman, and Rina Resurreccion

FOR SUE

on whose kitchen table
this memoir, gratefully, was written

Table of Contents

INTRODUCTION

T HIS MEMOIR COVERS A LOT of my living time: from the
mid-1930s through today, over eighty years. When I
was born, in 1934, my family and most others were digging
themselves out of the Great Depression; much of the worst
was yet to come.

Recent literary memoirs have mostly been by women trying to tease out the links between their lives as lived and their
lives as they commit them to text. Men have similar struggles,
and have begun to explore their personal travails and triumphs in their work with their readers — as I have done in
my memoir here.

My memories, supported by letters and other family documents, carry me from birth to the present. This is a long
stretch of life in a rapidly evolving world. In this memoir I
have struggled to report my encounters with the world, in
what has not been a happy life. Bed-wetting, a nasty mother,
and impotence have dragged me down as I have struggled to
persevere.

I have partially succeeded, and I believe my successes will

be of interest and perhaps inspiration to the very many other men who have been ambushed by life and are trying to overcome similar defaults. My memoir even has a happy ending!

Much of my progress has been due to psychoanalysis, which has given me mental access to forgotten events and emotions from long ago. I hope my readers will be inspired by a sense of kinship. We are not alone in our unsightly struggles!

This is my message.

Let me note that I have been a professional writer for all of my career. I have written and published half a dozen nonfiction books, mostly on scientists and doctors.

This is my only memoir. I am unaware of any memoir by any other writer on the subjects I have covered here.

THIS IS A TRUE STORY about how a wondrously unique animal sustained my life — but imprisoned me within myself. And, it is a report on how I have struggled to free myself!

I did not set out to write a memoir here. I had no horn to toot. But: You have to know something about something in order to write about it. And now I am the only subject left that I know enough about to write about. So, I am doing it here. I do remember and know a lot about myself.

The main themes, the major lifelong crises in my life, have been dealing with two devastating problems: bed-wetting and impotence. They shamed and embarrassed me all the time. They still do.

Bed-wetting manifested itself before I was five and continued until I was seventeen. Impotence, in the same organs — brain and penis — became apparent in my late teens and has never abated, despite fourteen years of psychoanalysis and additional years of psychotherapy. The relationship between these two life curses has never been clear to me. But it seems likely that they are in fact related.

I first became keenly aware of my bed-wetting "problem" in the spring of 1939, when I was five. I had been "dry" for a while. I remember getting into bed with my father and mother in their bed on Sunday mornings. It was warm and comfortable. No mishap occurred. But then, one Sunday morning, I dozed off. When I awoke, I discovered that I had let go, fouling the bed — and profoundly irritating my father. I never again was invited back on a Sunday morning.

The thing about bed-wetting was that, while I might not want to do it, that wish never reached the parts of myself and my body that actually were doing it (or paid no attention to my wishes). Those parts of me were unreachable, always. There was no way I could engage them with my conscious mind. So I avoided trying to think about them. My effort went instead to trying to hide and deny what I was doing to friends who discovered it through the smell and the sight of my stained sheets.

My other penile disaster, which I became aware of in my teens, is impotence: I couldn't get it up. I had been terribly afraid of girls, whom I also was terribly attracted to. If I interacted with them, I feared they would cut me off. Dismiss me as nothing. I might see or even smell a girl. But if I spoke to her, I would reveal my weakness, my unworthiness. The more beautiful she appeared to me, the more I was attracted to her — and the more dire her riposte would be if I tried to enter her realm, and, therefore, I imagined, the more devastating the rebuff. As I understand it, screwing her was my ultimate goal. I didn't know what that meant. But it was also my ultimate fear. I had no idea that a girl could like me, could want me. . . .

I finally came face to face with my problem as I was leaving college at Brandeis University. It was June 1955. I was graduating. A senior dance was to be held at a hotel in Boston. With great trepidation, I invited a classmate. On our way home in my car, we stopped at a deserted place, a football stadium in Waltham. The red roses in the Waltham house fronts were in bloom. I remember that.

We walked. We stopped. We kissed. I went forward on automatic pilot. She did not resist.

We were undressed. I was on top of her. My penis was limp. There was no way I could penetrate her. Nor could I come. Nor could I pleasure her.

After five minutes of trying, we stopped. She said, "Not to worry! It happens!" But my worry was already focused. It has remained focused ever since. Like bed-wetting. I had no access to my feeling or ability to think about what went wrong. I couldn't change my feelings or understand them. I was cast out of myself.

We watched the sun come up. But we never spoke about what had happened. I still recoil in shame when I hear her name. I don't recall if I've seen her since! I think that I did, once or twice.

In both enuresis and impotence, my penis wasn't doing what it was supposed to do. My penis, I realized only later, in therapy, was not my mother's favorite organ. Quite the contrary.

When I was younger in my thinking, my job was reporting for doctors in a news magazine, *Medical World News*; I was paid to keep ahead of events and developments in medicine and science. I was *au courant* and so knew of many new and reportable developments as they occurred. This also positioned me to write about health for the *Ladies' Home Journal*, a women's magazine, and take on freelance assignments. This work led me into my first book, *Rh*. But as I got deeper into *Rh* — it was a several-year project — I got further away from the breaking news. Fortunately, I still had the *Journal* for which to stay current.

Then, my anger about pesticides' destructiveness of wild life led me into peregrine falcons and other birds — and I had a news beat again. I followed it for a decade. Eventually it was too narrow to sustain a career.

Later, I turned to *Sankofa*, which is about misconduct in black-led research on a slave cemetery in Manhattan. I allowed myself to believe that my exposé and my writing would attract readers. I was dead wrong. I ignored advice from my agent, and from colleagues and friends, that this was not a topic that would command wide interest. I pressed on. By the time I finished the book, after more than a decade, I knew a whole lot about the African Burial Project and its participants and problems. I probably knew more about it, and why it failed, than anyone else. But by then I no longer had any working knowledge about any other topic. So when it was finished, and there were no follow-up assignments, my well had run dry.

Complicating this narrowed focus was my moving from New York City to Northern Vermont, where I couldn't find anything to cover — no research — nor any publication to write for. I was foundering. I wrote some desultory local news articles. But I did want to continue writing — and the only topic left that I knew enough about to write about was me!

Let me note that what follows was mostly written from memory. And memory is fallible. So I apologize here, in advance, for the mistakes I have made.

So here is the result: the book you are holding. You will be the judge of whether I have entertained and informed you.

—D.Z.,
Sheffield, VT

HARBINGER

A VERY ATTRACTIVE GIRL in my fifth grade class at Chicago's Kenwood Public School invited me to a party. In a conspiratorial tone of voice, she gave me directions to her home, not far from my own.

Conveniently, her parents were out for the evening. The party's purpose, she explained to the nine or ten boys and girls present, was to play Spin the Bottle: We sat in a circle on her living room floor. One person would spin a bottle at the center of the circle. When it stopped spinning — when it came to rest — the bottle's mouth faced a girl or a boy in the circle. Then, the spinner and the selected person, always a boy and a girl, would stand up, go to an adjacent small parlor, and shut the door. There, they could kiss each other in private. Everyone else listened from the living room for clues to what they were doing. We tried to imagine from the sounds and lapsed times what the lucky pair were up to. It was awkward, but it was compelling.

I must have been picked out by the bottle a couple of times

— and I kissed partners in the parlor. I don't remember how it felt, but I performed well enough to be invited back.

Then, at one of these parties I went into the parlor with a different girl — I forget who she was. But instead of kissing and being kissed by her, I kissed the back of my hand. Loudly and longly. I told her to do the same. After several minutes we rejoined the circle, whose members might have wondered what we had been up to. Were we hot together?

Not at all!

That evening was the last in my Spin-the-Bottle career. I had no more party invitations. Later, I came to realize that my effort had not been to learn how to kiss and enjoy it. Rather, I followed my feelings — which were to fake it. I became embarrassed and dismayed by my reticence and my reluctance to play by the Spin-the-Bottle rules. I still am dismayed today. I was faking things instead of searching the pleasures that the party was set up to initiate. I wondered despairingly why I acted as I had.

Why? For one thing, my initial kissing experiences, I now remember, did not bring me pleasure, or even the promise of pleasure. So, unmotivated, I mockingly did what the game prescribed: I produced a myriad of kisses, all of them fake.

Was I renouncing pleasure? I don't think so. Somewhere beyond the game we were playing, I must have felt, there was another, true source of pleasure for me. Sooner or later I would experience it. But I never have.

The Spin-the-Bottle episode can be called "harbinger."

I

TEXAN UNDERPINNINGS

M Y GOOSE WAS COOKED before I was born. My wad was shot, to invoke another metaphor that signifies that major directions my life would take were in place before I could even be aware of them.

I know this because, fortuitously, my mother's eldest sister, my aunt Esther Radoff-Perl, wrote a family history in 1961, and I have in hand one of the few typescript copies. According to this record, my grandparents on my mother's side arrived in America in the 1880s and '90s. They came from Lithuania. In my mother's family the story was that one of them — my grandmother I believe, but I'm not sure — was descended from a famous Jewish wise man of the city of Vilna, the *Vilna Gaon*. Maybe this is true, maybe not; many Lithuanian Jewish families claim him as their own!

Aunt Esther wrote ostensibly to tell her daughter, Harriett, me, my sister Judy, and the one other cousin in our generation what a fine and accomplished woman my grandmother Nennie Rabinowitz, or *Goldie* as she was called, had been. But the MS also is a history of the Radoff family, and it reveals much about my mother Sarah: It describes the forces in the family that largely determined who she became.

Nennie was extraordinary, Esther writes. She was Jewish mother, an immigrant from Stuchen, in Grodno province in the Russian empire, and an early settler in Houston. And she was family breadwinner at times. She made her children's clothes, including the "fancy work" for her daughters' wool and silk dresses. She was observant, ran a kosher household, and ministered to the needs of tenants and neighbors, black and white, Esther recounts. Nennie was an exemplary and unusually civic-minded woman: "She must have been of Herculean stuff. . . . Besides taking care of the children, the house, the garden, the [newly immigrated] 'green' relatives, the cow — which she milked twice a day — and the poultry, she also had roomers and boarders. . . . She found time to serve on the ladies' committees of the annual Purim and Chanukah balls. . . . [O]n Sundays and evenings she had the use of the family's delivery horse. . . . Mama would hitch him up to the. . .'buggy' . . .and take the family out for a drive." Later, Nennie reportedly was the first Houston woman to have a driver's license.

My mother's first misfortune was the order of her birth. Like many immigrant families, the Radoffs wanted boys. But Esther, number one, was a girl — and also quite bright and able. Number two was another girl, Anne. She was beautiful. Then, finally, came a boy, Jacob. But he died at age two from diphtheria.

Still, no surviving boys.

Then came my mother Sarah, in July 1902. Still *another* girl. Esther has little to report about her, and in her long MS, Sarah is rarely mentioned, usually only in passing. Her lack of standing was confirmed by Nennie's last two babies: Leon and David were the long-sought males.

MY MATERNAL GRANDFATHER, HARRY, was born in or near Grodno, in about 1865. The family was poor, and its members did not get along well with each other. So Harry left home at age thirteen and worked his way west through Europe. In London, he labored in a sweat shop, learned English, and saved enough money to buy a transatlantic ticket, as did his brother, Henry. They went to Johnstown, Pennsylvania, where they opened a picture-framing store. Harry was almost drowned when the great Johnstown Flood of 1888 washed the shop away. He then moved first to Greensburg, Pennsylvania, then to Houston, Texas, with his newlywed wife Nennie. It was not to be a happy marriage.

Harry was well versed in Yiddish and Hebrew, and was a sometime rabbi, according to Esther. But he also was an irascible, intemperate rogue.

Papa wasn't an easy husband to get along with, Esther writes, and Mama also had her faults. So they had their arguments and quarrels, and sometimes he would refuse to speak to her. "He'd come home for his meals. . .but if he had to communicate anything to her, he would tell it to me or one of the others: 'Tell Mama so and so. . . .'"

Houston was a more prosperous place than Greensburg. The family reopened their business, which grew rapidly. They named it Radoff Brothers and developed it into a department store. But the brothers disagreed about business and occasionally came to blows. "After these fights," Esther reports, "Papa would come home all bloodied and bruised, vowing not to return to the store. But he always did."

This friction never abated, and finally, in 1917, Uncle Henry bought Harry out after much aggravation and conflict.

"Papa was very hard to get along with, so [the quarrel] was probably more his fault than Uncle Henry's. . . . He had a very quick, hot temper; he was opinionated, conceited, and intolerant, especially of changes. . . . He was 'the boss' and never spent a penny on the [girls]. . . . But Papa didn't mind spending money on [his sons] Leon and David. [He] really indulged them so much that they were quite spoiled."

Nennie, who had arrived in the U.S. in 1892, was not a hugger. Esther describes her "peculiarity": a "lack of demonstrativeness as far as affection was concerned. She was naturally reserved and didn't display her emotions. This made her seem cold and unloving. I never saw any sign of affection between her and my father. . . .

"When I reached the age [when] mothers start thinking of their daughters' social life, [she and papa] really disagreed most of the time. Young men who might have dated my sister Anne and me were actually afraid to come [by] at night."

The way my mother, Sarah, told it, her father was a womanizer and a drunk. My mother saw this, and she saw my grandmother's rage against him.

The chaos in the family, and the conflict between Harry and Nennie, grew worse and worse. It reached a crescendo when Nennie walked out on him. She returned only when reconciliation was arranged by family members and friends. They moved back in together, in a new house, but remained at loggerheads. He would leave home early in the morning and return late at night, after everyone else had gone to bed. In between, in the evenings, he spent much of his time at the nearby home of a widow, Mrs. Dorfman.

"Papa spent a good many of his evenings at her place," Esther writes. "Naturally this started scandalous talk, which came back to Mama and upset her very much."

Harry disinherited his family.

Sarah, my mother, was an adolescent when this was going on. Siding with her mother may have led her to dislike men. Scarier perhaps, my sister Judy believes that Harry molested my mother in this period.

She bases this view on a dream — a nightmare actually — that Sarah reported to her around the time of her eighty-fifth birthday in 1988. In this dream, Sarah was being sexually accosted by her father. If this dream reflects fact, as Judy believes, it must have made a strong impression on my mother to be remembered, vividly, some seventy years later.

Judy also notes that Sarah came to deny her father's presence in her life during her own adolescence. She indicated that he died in about 1912, when Sarah was ten. In fact, he passed away, after a major stroke, at about the time she left home for college in 1920. She certainly never mentioned him to me.

I don't know a lot about Sarah's life as she grew up and left home. She attended the University of Texas. Then she moved to Chicago but came back to Texas after a year because of the cold. She graduated from Rice University. She lived, at least for a while, at Jane Adam's Hull House, in Chicago, but according to an interview conducted late in her life, she does not appear to have been part of the women's rights and socialist movements that grew up there.

In Chicago, Sarah worked at a brokerage and joined a choral group. It was at this time, in the early 1920s, that she met my father, whom everyone called *Zim*. He had changed his name from Lieb Moishe to *Leo*. She came to be called *Sally* instead of Sarah (and I will respect that change here). They both had outgrown their immigrant origins to become thoroughly Americanized middle-class strivers, pursuers of the American Dream. Remarkably, the children of both families attended college. They celebrated the Jewish Holy High Days with his family in Indiana Harbor and, later, on Chicago's South Side. But they lived secular lives. They were wed in 1924.

I was born August 10, 1934, in the midst of the Depression. I do know that Zim had a surgical practice where he cared for workers from the Chicago Stockyards who were injured on the job. He had enough work that they were not severely threatened by the Great Depression. I know far less about Zim's early life than I do about Sally's. His family had moved to Indiana Harbor, near the Illinois border. Like the Radoffs, they ran a store. Zim was the second of eight children, and the only son who did not go into business. He appears to have been his mother's favorite, and her fear of cancer may have influenced his choice of a medical and surgical career.

He earned his M.D. at Rush Medical College in Chicago. Later he spent some of postgraduate work in Germany in the early 1920s.

2

MOM 'N' ME

MY RELATIONSHIP WITH MY MOTHER was quite fractious. No doubt I baited her. But there can be no doubt that she attacked me emotionally and physically.

In Chicago, when I was a teen, we would get into an argument in, say, the kitchen. All of a sudden, I would be running, and she would be chasing me 'round the house, swinging a broom. Through the dining room and living room, up the front stairs, then to the back, down the rear stairs, and into the kitchen. Round and round we went. Sometimes back to front, sometimes front to back — the broom flailing behind me.

It dawned on me that this wasn't a game. She was out to hurt me! Fortunately, I had a sanctuary: The bathroom outside my bedroom had a secure door lock. You slammed the door, then quickly turned a dial, and a bar slid into the door frame. She could rattle the door. But the lock always held. I feared she would break down the door. She never did.

The bathroom was my refuge. I was often cold. So I would undress and slip into the tub. I could lie back and work the faucets with my feet. I had books there and would pass the time reading. I would drain the tub and lie in the warmth radiating from the enamel. It was there, shielded from my mother's rage by a solidly locked door, that I discovered masturbation. In retrospect, it was a fraught way to discover sex.

MY MOTHER WAS ANTAGONISTIC toward my father and all men, toward sex, and toward motherhood, members of my father's family later told me. She didn't want to become pregnant with my younger sister, and had to be chivied along by Zim and his mom, my grandmother. Did she want to become pregnant with me — that's a good question given the nine year interval between their wedding in 1924 and my conception in late 1933.

My parents appear to have successfully made the transition from immigrants' children to full-fledged — striving — Americans in the short time span of a single generation; witness their names: Sarah more and more came to be called *Sally*. My father's given name was *Leib Moishe*. He anglicized it to *Leo*, and kept the middle initial *M*. Everyone in his family called him *Zim*.

I had a sense, never confirmed, that my mother was latently gay. She became attracted to Zim when her friend, his sister Lillian, got married — and she found herself lonely. Lillian had fixed her up with Zim, and my mother may have felt he was her best option. This is conjecture.

Sally had romantic dreams. She spoke often of her warm impressions of Howard Mumford Jones, a popular author and lecturer of the time. Was this a romance or a fantasy crush? I think the latter.

After I was born, my mother joined a child study group associated with the University of Chicago. Its purpose was to help parents relate to their infants by watching the babies and making notes on their observations. Fortunately for this memoir, I still have my Baby Book, in which she wrote down her observations of me. My developmental milestones and behaviors are carefully noted in it.

This methodology, as I understand it, emphasized *watching* the baby, to the detriment of experiencing it, *holding* and *loving* it. I think the loneliness I long have felt in part grew out of this hands off isolation.

I was fairly okay at birth. But by age three problems had begun to arise: bed-wetting, timidity, fear of loud noises. *Began wetting pants at nursery school. Wouldn't eat food given to him. Timidity has given way to 'toughness', meanness and some bullying,* reads her entry in the Baby Book. But, to Sally, I seemed well adjusted.

A terrific fear of loud noises — motorcycles, trains —

always present but getting worse toward his third birthday.

These are prescient observations. In my eighties, I still fear loud noises, and swimming in cold water — and bed-wetting — shaped who I am.

You often see photos of babies being bounced on their mothers' laps. They hold each other. They smell each other. They are "digging" each other, as my jazz friends would say. This is what did *not* happen to me. My mother and I had very few such bonds. When, later, I was with a woman, I never felt the pull of erotic attraction that I could respond to with my own. I felt that there was no one there for me. I think I am impotent in part for want of these feelings. My mother seems not to have had loving feelings toward me that I might have reciprocated to her and to all the other "hers" that I encountered later.

Rather, I felt distance and impenetrability in my fantasies about girls and women. Sometimes, what is more, I felt a hateful disinterest from my mother. One instance, when I was four or five, occurred at a beach in the Indiana Sand Dunes.

She and I were playing in the shallows. I held my breath and ducked under the water. My mother was right next to me. As I started to surface, I could feel her holding me. Then I realized she *was* holding me down. Under the water!

I struggled and she let me go, and let me up. I scampered onto the beach. I realized, and I have *never* forgotten, that my mother was trying to push my head down under the water.

A second, similar scare came a few years later. During World War II, we were living in a rental house in Seattle, Washington. My mother was in the kitchen. I was outside playing with some neighborhood boys. We were on top of our flat-roofed car garage when, suddenly, they seized me, and hung me out over the ground some fifteen feet below. I screamed. Finally, I escaped back into the kitchen. I tearfully told my mother what had happened.

No sympathy!

If she said anything, it was to tell me to go back outside — which I refused to do.

A third such episode: We were living in Los Angeles then, a few years later. I thought I was friendly with the local boys. But one day, I'm talking to them on the street when, suddenly, I'm running away, and they are chasing me. One threw a pocket knife; it bounced off my back. When I made it home, my mother had no sympathy whatsoever for my plight, my fear.

At best, my life was no longer her concern. My fear was not her worry. I was, at age ten, emotionally on my own.

She didn't care about me one way or the other.

3

SNOOKY / SANTHI

THIS IS AN ACCOUNT OF THE MOST IMPORTANT relationship in my life.

My bedtime routine when I was a toddler was for the maid to get me bathed and ready for sleep. My mother then would come into my room. Sometimes, she soothed me by rubbing my back. This was the one comforting physical action that I remember her doing for me. Then, we said my prayers. One was in Hebrew. One was in English: "We thank thee now, O God our King, who rest to us at night doth bring, and makes the sleep fall on our eyes, safe in thy care the whole world lies." How terrible, given what already was happening to Jews in Germany. Then I hugged Snooky and went to sleep.

Snooky was a much-handled, much-fondled doggy. He was white, and most of his hair was gone (I must have hugged him a lot). He had a well-loved appearance. He had come to me as a present on my first birthday. (My mother had noted the arrival of this "wooly dog, which he loved at once," in my Baby Book.)

I remember my mother telling me one evening when I was three that this would be my last night with Snooky. He had served his purpose, she said, and now it was time for him to go away so I could put myself to sleep. I think I tried to protest. But I couldn't say much of anything. Perhaps I was choked up. I am less certain that I remember the next bedtime, when Snooky no longer was with me. His end, I believe, was one of my earliest self-conscious moments.

I don't remember how I reacted, internally, to Snooky's demise — his death in my life, as it were. But in the preceding months, I must have clung to him forcefully. Was my mother jealous of Snooky?

As time went by, Snooky left my conscious memory. I forgot about him. But he lingered on in my unconscious.

I came down with scarlet fever in the winter of 1940. I was somewhat delirious. So my memory of this time is not as sharp as I would wish. While I was ill, I was given a story book about a cat who was searching for a tail. I assume now that was because he had been born tailless — a manx cat — like my present cat "Stubby," who is sitting with me here as I write this. *Stubs, Stubby!*

The storybook cat was led on by the people and animals he knew or met in his quest. I remember that one of his excursions was to a swamp, where he found and collected *cat-tails*. But these plants were not what he needed.

I forget the rest of the story, and sadly, the name of the book — for I would like to find and re-read it. But the message was clear: If the cat in the story found one new tail, perhaps he could find two, and would give one to me. Clearly I had a penis problem.

Helina Martinez

Fast forward now thirty years. I am in psychoanalysis. I had never written a children's story (nor have I written one since). But I began to want to write a story about a mythical animal, one who lived far away, in the magical palace of an Eastern Great Prince.

I couldn't put this animal out of my head. I imagined him — it was a *him* — in many shapes and guises. He was furry. He was white. He walked upright on his back legs. He was friendly. He was especially friendly toward a little boy, Danny, who encountered him. Since he was a "wild" animal, he lived out-of-doors, in the Great Prince's royal garden. What were his identifying characteristics? How was he different, say, from Winnie the Pooh and the many other benign animals that inhabit children's stories.

Well, simple. This animal had not one, but *two* furry tails. Two tails! One for himself, and the other one perhaps for me, in need of a functional appendage. His name? Since he was a unique animal, he needed a unique name. An oriental-sounding name. I encouraged possible names to trip across my tongue — and finally settled on *Santhi*, after convincing myself that it was a singular name, one that would not lead me into a later conflict with another author or a publisher claiming plagarism.

Later, after the story was finished, I recognized that Santhi in reality had been *Snooky*. The child in the story, Danny, of course was me. And I identified the facilitator, the Great Prince in whose garden Danny met Santhi, as my psychoanalyst, Dr. Emanuel Peterfreund.

It soon turned out that Santhi did not live just on the page: He was alive *inside* me! In my mind. I found that I could invoke him, bring him into consciousness, even talk to him!

How could that be? The simple — but frightening — answer I discovered was this: *My* inner being *was* Santhi.

I want to avoid technical words in this account, but Santhi was — is — my *id*, my living vital self. My feelings as it were.

To simplify the matter, I can say that Santhi was and is my — David's — *inside*. The part of me that talks, writes, lives with other people in the world, what technically can be called my *ego*, can be more simply understood as my *outside*. "I" — my outside — is taking care of my inside, Santhi!

I found that I could bring Santhi into consciousness by calling him in a wounded way, "*Santhi, Santhi, Santhi....*" When he arrived, he warmed my heart! "Oh, Santhi," I would say. In so doing, I was reunited again with my long lost Snooky.

When do I invoke Santhi, bring him up into consciousness? When I see or experience something of remarkable beauty. Or, more specifically, when I encounter something of remarkable beauty that is threatened by death. "*Santhi, Santhi, Santhi...* " I will intone when someone in a book or in the news is threatened. "Help her," or "him," I will implore Santhi. We both want to help — but we feel that we are helpless to do so.

I have discussed Santhi in therapy with two psychoanalysts. Neither offered to interpret him, leaving that task to me. Santhi may have saved my life. But for my insides, my *id*, to be given over to him also has had *catastrophic* results for me.

I must have internalized Snooky/Santhi out of deep fear of loneliness and death when I was very young, perhaps around the time my mother removed Snooky from my bed and discarded him. There was trauma there, no doubt, but exactly how it came down in time, I am unable to say. What I know is *I* am Santhi. Santhi is *me.* But with Santhi inhabiting my inner self, there was no way for me, *David,* to grow, mature, along with my outer part. Emotionally, I never grew beyond infancy, age three or four say. Santhi *is* David, dead to the world.

This might account in part for my bed-wetting; I was still an infant inside. It also may account for my failure to grow emotionally. To my clumsiness in boyhood games. My lack of skill and surety compared, say, to my friend Jessie Cook. When I was just coming out of my years of sickness, Jessie was a skilled softball player. I couldn't catch the ball!

Sometimes, when I invoke Santhi, I have the impression that I'm, say, a seven-year-old boy talking to a three-year-old younger brother. Santhi was something (someone) to hold onto, something that made it possible for my life to advance. But at a terrible price. I was alienated from my human feelings. The part of me that could love and relate to another person was tied up — locked away — in my fantasy animal. I had locked my emotional center (id) inside myself as another living being, called *Santhi.* These essential feelings were not available to me in reality. I was locked in and at the same time locked out of myself. This became my way of life.

I soon forgot about Snooky. I did not rediscover him for thirty-some years, in psychoanalysis, when I felt the urge to write about "Santhi." Snooky and Santhi certainly are one. To this day, at age eighty-five, it is only by invoking Santhi — by saying his name, by talking to him — that I experience feelings of love, awe, and death.

I now invoke Santhi in poignant moments — when death threatens life. For me, the *Swan Lake* music — where the lovely swan maidens are attacked by the evil sorcerer Von Rothbart — is the most poignant, the most moving, moment of all. I weep. Eros defeated. Eros killed.

"Santhi!" I gasp. *"Santhi!"*

It is my most emotional moment.

I am beholden to my fantasy companion. I am not similarly beholden to any aspect of reality. This is how I have lived — the best of it — for eighty years. Santhi keeps me alive. Santhi keeps me alone!

What is the relationship of Snooky and Santhi? Snooky, after all, is a dog. A toy dog. Santhi, on the other hand, is an exotic animal who stands up straight and looks like a cross between a rabbit and a small bear. The most important difference is their tails: Snooky had one. Santhi has two.

He is the only animal in the world with two tails. Why? Bluntly, I believe, because one tail is for Santhi. The other, figuratively speaking, is for me.

I began my search for a new appendage a few years later, when I was sick with scarlet fever. The new appendage that I sought, I am sure, was a penis. I don't know how I sensed that. But I believe that that was so.

When Santhi first appeared in my consciousness, I decided to write a story about him. I didn't yet understand his importance. I still was focused on my need for a cure for my impotence. Anything less felt like a distraction: giving up, as it were. Yet Santhi has turned out to be the key to my personality and my life. Clearly, without psychoanalysis I would never have recovered him.

Is it better to know than not to know?

So, *faut de mieux*, I have discovered much about my life that otherwise would have remained hidden inside me. I now know more or less what went wrong. I am better off for that knowledge, though still deeply disappointed that it did not lead to the cure I desperately sought.

4

SURROGATES

WHILE MY RELATIONSHIP WITH MY MOTHER always was fraught, I fortunately did develop through the years very close relationships with several other adults. They were, as I recognized only much later, *surrogates* for my parents. These were indeed life-saving, life-sustaining relationships for me.

The first, when I was twelve or thirteen, was with a young psychologist-in-training from St. Louis, who soon afterward became my *Aunt Gibby*. (Her family name was Gibbstein.) The second, a few years later, was our family cook, Robena Jackson. She was a black woman out of the South, who came to Chicago during the great exodus to the North that has come to be called the Great Migration. The third, when I was in college, was a butcher in Boston, who had won a camera in a raffle, learned to use it, and become the official Brandeis University photographer — and is a much revered figure there to this day.

My Aunt Gibby was engaged to my father's younger brother Alvin. She lived in a large house half a mile west of us along Fifty-second Street, where she had started her psychological practice. It was decided — how I do not know — that I should see her professionally. I, of course, had no idea what a therapist did; I saw Gibby as a family member and friend.

Visiting her, on Saturday mornings, was a big deal for me, since I had to walk west on Fifty-second Street and cross several streets, one of which, Woodlawn Avenue, was a through street. This meant that cars could keep going and did not have to stop for pedestrians at the crosswalks. I learned to navigate this route.

Gibby and I talked. We schmoozed. We painted together with watercolors. She was an artist, and we made paintings of bowls and other objects in her flat. Later she framed some of her own pictures for the walls of her home. When she died, I asked her children for one of them. It hangs in my home today. (I realized only recently that it was a paint-by-number work.) Gibby and I had fun together. Then, in the early afternoon, after lunch, I would put on my coat and go home.

I remained infatuated with Gibby as she married my uncle Alvin. They moved into the Blackwood, a twelve-story apartment building right behind my backyard. I would go looking for her there. These excursions were not approved. But we remained very close to each other all of her life. I miss her badly now that she is gone. I loved her. She reciprocated my feelings.

MY SECOND SURROGATE, ROBENA JACKSON, would be cooking when I came home from school by climbing over the back fence and coming in through the kitchen door. I would sit on the radiator — I always seemed to be chilly — and we would talk while she was working. We talked about all sorts of things, including my mother, whom Robena disliked.

Through our time together, I became interested in cooking. But I don't recall that Mrs. Jackson provided any lessons, albeit she was a fabulous cook and baker; she made chocolate cakes that I can savor to this day. The thing about Robena was that she was not judgmental of me, although she of course knew that I wet my bed. It was our one-on-one relationship that made her so precious to me.

Years later, she moved to Los Angeles to be near her daughters. When she died, I flew there for her funeral.

RALPH NORMAN, THE BRANDEIS school photographer, like Robena, similarly met me person-to-person; he, like Robena, was not judgmental.

I was a photographer when I went to Brandeis. So it was only natural that I sought student employment with

Ralph. The first thing that I did was carry the "slave unit," a flash gun detached from his camera that I would aim at the person whose picture he was taking. The flash from his camera would trigger the slave unit's flash, and the side light it provided lent depth to the shot. Soon, I started working in his industrial-sized darkroom, developing film and printing pictures on the enlarger, to fill the demand for Ralph's work.

Ralph never judged me and rarely complained about the work I was doing. He was a congenial man and got along well with athletes, social climbers, artists, and most if not all of the other groups of students and faculty on campus.

Ralph loved to eat, as I do. Often, after a photo shoot, we would repair to a restaurant in Waltham for lunch or dinner. His favorite was a delicatessen on Main Street that served derma, borscht, corned beef, and other Jewish dishes. Ralph was friendly with the staff. Indeed, he was friendly with just about every person who came into the place. He was not an angry man.

My work with Ralph changed in my second year. A new student employee came aboard, who was an exceptionally fine photographer: Henry Grossman. He was breathtakingly good at what he was doing with his 35-mm camera. I felt unable to match or compete with the work he provided.

We became good friends and have remained so for sixty some years. Henry has won wide honors for his work: He took the inauguration photos of John F. Kennedy, which were also used on page one of the *New York Times* when JFK died. Henry photographed Eleanor Roosevelt and made her look handsome. He was — is — a consummate professional, and I am proud that he took the author photos for my books.

Ralph Norman was a musician. He played bongos, of all things, and searched opportunities to sit in with local Latin musical groups. One young black musician he came to know was called "Red." We visited Red at his gigs, and Ralph brought him to Brandeis to play for the students. Later, "Red" came out publicly as the racist black power leader calling himself *Malcolm X*. He became a rabble-rousing activist in Boston and New York. But he returned to Brandeis one last time, at Ralph's invitation, to play for the students.

ONE OTHER PERSON, IN FACT TWO OF THEM, a married couple, had been straight and kindly with me. They were my mother's younger brother, Leon Radoff — *Uncle Leon* to me — and his wife *Aunt May*. I know nothing about Leon's childhood, at a time when his mother and father were increasingly at odds with each other. But it could not have been pleasant in my grandmother's den of man-haters.

Leon and May were my surrogate parents. I was their surrogate son.

I came to know Leon and May in the late 1940s. My

mother, my sister Judy, and I went to stay with them, because of their proximity to the John Hopkins University Hospital in Baltimore. The reason for our visits: My sister Judy had been born, in 1939, with a congenital malformation of her heart called a *patent ductus arteriosus*. What this means is that an opening between the heart and the aorta that balances blood pressure in that organ occurs normally during fetal life but fails to close at birth, as it is supposed to. A range of cardiac symptoms, and eventually death, may result.

When Judy was born, the first experimental operation to close this duct had just been reported. This meant essentially that no treatment was yet available.

Zim kept this bad news to himself. He didn't tell our mother of Judy's risk. Neither, more understandingly, did he tell Judy. But for whatever reason — because of medical caution, fear, or because our family was out of balance because of the World War, he apparently did not act on the basis of what he knew.

A decade later, however, when Judy was about nine years old, corrective surgery had been invented. Zim told my mother about Judy's condition and said it was time to do the operation. Judy recalls that Sally didn't believe her surgeon husband! Angrily, she said she was determined to take Judy to Johns Hopkins, where she was sure that an extraordinary heart doctor, Helen Taussig, would tell her that Zim was wrong.

Dr. Taussic took X-rays and performed other tests. Based on them, she told my mother that it was *she* who was wrong. Zim was right.

Zim decided that Dr. Percival Potts, at Chicago's Children's Memorial Hospital, would do the operation. Through all of this *sturm and drang*, both parents failed to tell Judy what she faced. Judy recalls that when she was brought into Potts' office, he asked her if she knew why she was there. She replied, "No!"

Judy was operated on when she was ten. The surgery was successful; she has thrived ever since. She and our mother and I returned once or twice to Uncle Leon's, so that Dr. Taussic could perform follow-up studies. I don't recall that Zim ever came along.

Meanwhile, on our several visits to Maryland, I came to like Leon and May more and more — and they liked me. They were childless, and I was the closest thing to a son that they had.

Leon had gone to college in North Carolina, and earned a Ph.D. in English Literature. By then it was the Great Depression. Leon couldn't find work. What is more, he was told at Johns Hopkins, where he wanted to teach, that since he was Jewish, there was no chance that he would be hired there. Or anywhere, it seems, because Jews were not welcomed in English departments of American universities in the 1930s.

Leon's luck finally changed: The Commonwealth of

Maryland hired him as the State Archivist, the keeper of its governmental and historical papers and artifacts. He did well. Successive governors re-appointed him. Eventually he ruled over a large building, the Maryland Hall of Records, and a staff of assistants in Annapolis, Maryland's state capitol.

He had married May, a Christian woman, and they bought a seventeenth-century farm just outside Annapolis, near where the Bay Bridge now rises on the West to cross Chesapeake Bay to Maryland's Eastern Shore. Leon was a gentleman farmer. In the 1940s he and May had a good life for themselves with a local circle of friends.

It was with Leon and May that I first ate an oyster. In those days, oyster vendors parked their carts outside Baltimore's Union Train Station. So when Leon and May picked us up there on a visit, we could snack on fresh Chesapeake Bay oysters before we climbed into his car for the ride to Annapolis.

Besides his job for the State, Leon had crops in his fields and animals in his barn. He kept a dairy cow, which he named "Nennie" after his mother, my grandmother. Leon introduced me to a Southern, rural lifestyle — a white lifestyle — that was of course quite different, and certainly more interesting, than life on Dorchester Avenue.

We all gardened together. Leon grew luscious red tomatoes that he sliced into salads with onions and tarragon vinegar, which I've tried, but never succeeded, in duplicating. We ate blue crabs out of Chesapeake Bay. We fished in a nearby creek, and Leon pointed out water moccasins swimming silently through the reeds.

Leon was a hunter. He took me squirrel hunting. He carried the shotgun. Later, I stole several rifle bullets from his gun room, and sneaked them back to Chicago. I hung the bullets, one at a time, on wires in my clothes closet. Then I put a lit candle under them, and quickly closed the closet door. After what seemed like a long wait, they would explode with a satisfying *bang*.

My bed wetting continued at Leon's. But I think I felt less guilty about it when I was there. We certainly enjoyed each other's company!

After they died, I tried to claim their historic farm house as an inheritance. But, short of money at the end, Leon had sold it to the local school board in an irrevocable contract. The house has since been made into a historical museum.

5

TRAVEL

WE RODE THE GREEN DIAMOND, a flashy new Illinois Central streamliner, to Miami. We went first to one hotel, then quickly changed to another, the Roney Plaza, I believe. Were we forced to move because Jews were not welcomed at the first one? Possibly. But I'm not sure.

In our new hotel I would wake up very early each morning. I was allowed, indeed probably encouraged, to get dressed, leave the hotel room, go down the elevator to the lobby, and then step out on the boardwalk that ran between the hotels and the water. (This *board*walk was not made of wooden boards; it was asphalt.) The walk was lined with palm trees, and during the night tiny, immature coconuts would fall to the walkway. I collected lots of them and brought them back to the hotel room. (In walks around Wolf Lake, near Chicago, my father had taught me to collect "specimens" from nature.)

My guess is that these excursions provided my parents the private time they needed. My sister, Judy, was born the following September.

One day in Florida we took a ride on a glass-bottom boat. You could see the shallow bay floor through the glass and watch a swimmer pull up sponges, sea fans, and other specimens, which he brought up and presented to the passengers. I insisted that we keep a sea fan, which quickly stunk up the hotel bathroom, as I did the bed.

I became ill with a cold or flu. My parents decided to cut the vacation short. We returned to Chicago near New Year's Day in a regular steam train; the Green Diamond was sold out for the holidays.

At home, I recovered slowly. One afternoon, when my mother had gone downtown, I had a life-changing experience!

I was left with the maid. I awoke from my nap full of energy, eager to express my vim and vigor. I put my rideable metal toy horse up on my bed. I climbed on the seat and began rocking. The horse lurched forward. As it went off the end of the bed, I realized I was going down — a perception that stays in my memory.

I was soon lying on the floor in great pain, screaming and crying. My legs were tangled up in the horse. After what seemed like a long, long time, the maid came from the kitchen. I don't remember much of what happened, but I learned later that she was a Christian Scientist and had insisted, because this was their way, that I stand up and walk with her to the kitchen. Challenging the pain would make it better! She was wrong.

I could not stop crying with pain. Eventually, I roused our downstairs neighbor, Agnes Porges, who came up to see what was the matter. She phoned my father at his office downtown. He hurried home and quickly assessed that my left leg was broken. With my mother, who also had come home, he drove us to Michael Reese Hospital, where he was on staff. He carried me into a treatment room. I was by then hysterical, and my anguish only increased as my father held the evil-smelling either mask over my face. . . .

I remember that, when we came home from the hospital, I was accorded special privileges: Usually, I ate supper in the kitchen with the maid. But that night, when my father and mother sat down at the dining room table, I was brought in with them, and propped up in a chair. I was still in pain, and I didn't eat anything. Soon I was carried off to bed.

The next several months were a haze of pain and discomfort as my fractured left leg bone slowly mended. I kept being told that the cast would come off "soon." But "soon" seemed not to come. Finally, the heavy plaster cast was changed for a lighter, more flexible one. It allowed me to bathe and begin to move around the apartment. It was not until spring 1940 that I was somewhat up and about.

As I recuperated, my mother decided to visit her mother, my grandmother, at her home in Houston. On this trip, there was no Green Diamond. We took an ordinary steam train to St. Louis, where we had a layover before boarding a second train to Texas.

In the station, it was not clear where I should pee. If I went to the men's room, my mother couldn't come to help me with my clothes. But when I went with her to the ladies room, she felt embarrassed. Some friction with the other women in the room resulted.

The train we boarded, in coach, stopped in Dallas early the next morning, and we were told that there would be a twenty- or thirty-minute delay before it started again. We could get off briefly, and we deboarded in the train yard.

Then, all of a sudden, the train lurched forward and started to move without us. I think my mother screamed. Fortunately, after moving a short distance, the train stopped again, and we were able to scamper back on board. I was petrified. What if the train hadn't stopped but had kept going and left us alone in the Dallas train yard — forever?

In Houston, my mother was happy to be with her mother. They had much to say to each other, none of which I understood. I was let out of the house to play. My leg was still weak. I walked around the corner, where there were some shade trees, and sat down on the sidewalk. It was very hot.

Some broad-leafed green trees shaded the sidewalk. I

took shelter beneath them. Soon, I noticed several green-and-yellow caterpillars that had fallen from the trees onto the sidewalk. They were larger and more dramatically colored than the caterpillars at home in Chicago.

I picked several of them up and played with them! I allowed them to crawl over my hands, wrists, and arms.

The next day I brought a glass jar from my grandmother's kitchen. I trapped a couple of the insects and screwed down the jar lid above them, not neglecting to add a few leaves for them to eat. I poked some holes in the lid.

This play continued for several days, until it was time to go home. I told my mother and grandmother that I wanted to take these new pets home with me. They said no.

The jar was getting rather smelly by then, criss-crossed by strands of caterpillar cocoon silk. I insisted. They reiterated: *No.* Reluctantly, I took my jar back to the shaded sidewalk and tapped it until my caterpillars dropped out. Then we went to the train.

Just before my fifth birthday, we moved across the street, to 5205 Dorchester Avenue. This was (and is) a brownstone house, not an apartment like the one we had been living in. It had an urban backyard — a fenced-in rectangle of lawn and flower beds, that was perhaps thirty-by-sixty feet. My bedroom window at the back of the house looked out onto it.

There was a tree, a tall tree, midway between the two

side fences. It was quite straight, an elm tree perhaps. I liked looking at it.

One day my father said that the tree was going to be removed. Cut down. I don't recall that he said why. It didn't menace anyone; perhaps it had rot.

I was appalled. *Don't do it*, I must have said. But one day, I think when I was laid up in bed with scarlet fever, it was cut down.

While ill, I had built up a collection of toy animals: small, carefully reproduced lions, tigers, hippos, and rhinos, with elephants and monkeys, too. They were metal, cast lead, and they were light in weight because they were hollow. Their lead skins were paper thin.

I played with these animals often while sick in bed. I would arrange them on a board on the bed. But they broke easily. A leg would break off, or a gash would open up on an animal's flank. For verisimilitude, I wanted unbroken, that is to say *uninjured* animals, and my father and my uncle Harry, his brother, tried to oblige me. But, they said, they could not continue replacing these broken beasts, because they came from Germany — and had become hard to get because, as I learned later, of the Nazi takeover there and the resultant disruption in trade.

To meet the challenge of broken animals, I would set them up leaning on one another for stability, or next to a wooden block or other solid object. But that wasn't okay: They weren't natural.

At this time I had an all-day nurse. To protect my mother and my baby sister from catching scarlet fever, a fearsome and sometimes lethal disease, my mother did not come to my room in the back of the house. She and Judy stayed up front. I rarely saw them. I had the nurse instead.

She had a fix for broken animals that couldn't stand up by themselves. If one leg was missing, she would cut the other three off with scissors. So the hippo or the giraffe could stand up again, albeit on four severely foreshortened legs!

I protested. These animals with essentially no legs were no longer real to me. I removed the damaged beasts from my play. But the nurse, whose name I have forgotten, would not be deterred. Little by little, she cut down my menagerie — and I stopped playing with it.

Why have I remembered this so keenly? With the lead animals, as with the tree in the backyard, there was injury, which I seem to have experienced as castration. Cutting things down was the way of my world.

6

THE NEWS

H OW DID I GET INTERESTED in reading newspapers, and later, in writing for them?

In 1943, when I was nine, our my family lived in Seattle, Washington, where my father was a naval surgeon. This was a dramatic period in World War II, when the tide of battle began to shift toward the U.S. and the Allies.

Their progress — the ups and the downs — were front page news in the *Post-Intelligencer* and other Seattle papers. This coverage was highlighted with maps, often on Page One, showing troop and naval movements and battles with the Japanese in the Pacific, and with the Nazis in Europe. I read these reports — and became caught up in them.

Then, my mother, sister, and I followed my father by train to Oxnard (Port Hueneme), California, where Zim was assigned to embark with a medical care group, an

"Acorn," for the South Pacific. These preparations took a year. All this time, I kept up, and identified with the Allies' reported progress.

This interest continued when my mother, sister, and I returned to Chicago in 1944, while my father was overseas on the Pacific islands of Peleliu and Guam. Meanwhile, I became captivated by reporting in the Chicago newspapers of a sensational murder case: A five-year-old girl, Suzanne Degnan, had been kidnapped from her bedroom, and killed. Her body had been cut up, and the pieces distributed in sewer catch-basins near her home on the northwest side.

These gruesome discoveries continued for several days. Shortly thereafter the Chicago police arrested a young man, age seventeen, and charged him with the crime. What was unusual, and highly noteworthy, was that he was a college student at the University of Chicago. His name was William Heirens. The papers had a field day with his arrest, with Heirens' background (he came from a lower-class family), and with the trial, where he was found guilty of murder.

This was in a reprise of the Leopold-Loeb trial, several years earlier, for the murder of their young neighbor, Bobby Franks. Leopold and Loeb were also University of Chicago students, although unlike Heirens, they came from upper-crust Jewish families. It was a sensational case.

Heirens was sent to state prison. He spent the rest of his life there; he died in 2012. Because he was bright, and because of the notoriety of his crime, he became famous in the Illinois prison system. His achievements and setbacks were regularly reported in the newspapers. For decades he was the poster boy for crime and punishment in Chicago, and for life in the Big House.

Despite my absorption in the media, I did not then foresee myself as part of it. As I grew through childhood, in fact, I had little or no interest in what I was going to do when I grew up. Indeed, I had very little sense that I *was* growing up. I went along with what I had to do at school and at home. But, besides protecting myself physically from other boys, my mind drifted — and continues to do so today. I had a few friends, but I was not gregarious.

I have however remained an avid news reader. Only recently did it occur to me that that interest in the world, as presented by the press, established my relationship with the world outside myself and led eventually to my choice of journalism as a career. I see the world through newspapers.

7

CROSS CURRENTS

HOW DID I GET TO BE A REBEL? A revolutionary? I think that I now know:

When Santhi took over my id, I — David — could no longer relate pleasurably to anyone or anything outside of myself. I was locked in.

That meant that I found no pleasure in my family, or in virtually anyone or anything else. So I began to hate what I was urged to feel, but could not.

An example comes to mind. The Zimmermans were friendly with a suburban family, the Howard Adlers, whom we visited on Sunday afternoons. The Adlers' two girls were accomplished musicians, and would perform for guests.

My parents were quite attentive to their playing. I was not, because I could not be. I would lie on the floor with my body under a coffee table. Or I would say rude things. Eventually I would leave the living room, put on my coat, and walk to the back of the Adlers' property, where there were woods. There was a stream. I followed it up and down, splashing in the water and getting my feet wet. As the sun set, I returned to the musical recital in time for supper and the long car ride home. I had not heard the music but bad-mouthed it, which greatly annoyed my parents.

It was the same disdainful routine at the Art Institute. And in the movies. When a hunter killed Bambi's mother, I laughed. I was not feeling what others were; I attacked others' worlds.

Bed-wetting disrupted my socialization. I did not — could not — go on sleepovers with my friends. This added to my isolation at an age when overnight visits were important in widening kids' ambits beyond their immediate families.

How would I ever sleep with girls! That was unimaginable.

When, later, communism came into my life, I was altogether ready to overthrow the world that gave me no connectedness or happiness, and take a chance on a new world to come. (But I was far more interested in destroying the old order than I was in anticipating the new, revolutionary order — which I did not truly believe in.)

The acme of my disrespect came on a Saturday morning, while the temple members where we worshipped were conducting Sabbath services; religious school students were required to attend. Downstairs from the auditorium were men's and women's bathrooms, connected by a large storage room. I led several friends inside. I turned on the lights, and, while we smoked Lucky Strike and Philip Morris cigarettes we played poker.

The rabbi, Jacob Weinstein, eventually learned of my provocation and ordered this punishment: I was to read Thomas Mann's *Joseph in Egypt*. Which I did, sort of. (Years later, in New York, Jacob Weinstein married me and my first wife, Veva.)

My hidden Marxist education was complemented by an open and above-board acceptance of American democracy. This focus was course work at the University of Chicago, based on key American historical documents. They were presented in a two-volume green-covered set of books called *The People Shall Judge*. It traced the Colonies' rejection of British rule and the development of our democratic nation — racism and other faults included. They impressed me that this was who we were. So, confusingly, I now was a Marxist-Jeffersonian hybrid. It may seem odd now, but it made sense to me then.

An unanticipated opportunity to move forward in my life occurred in 1949, when I was in the ninth grade at the Lab School. I had volunteered to serve on the student council, since that provided a pass out of the classroom for one hour each week. Then, I was told that I was one of a few students eligible to run for the presidency of the council for the following year. Why not? I said to myself.

My two opponents were both better connected socially than I was.

One was the scion of a wealthy, well-established Jewish family — business people and philanthropists — on the South Side of Chicago. The other was a persnickety fellow who regularly greeted me, physically, with a wedgie —a sharp, and very hurtful jab to my upper arm — accompanied by caustic remarks.

My friend, Peter Gourfain, already an artist, helped me by painting a colorful poster: Vote Zimmerman.

I campaigned hard, and, to my surprise, I won!

I don't remember much about what I did as student council president. But it was an occasion for me to buy and read *Robert's Rules of Order*, the standard guide to parliamentary procedure. It showed me how the chairman could manage a deliberative assembly. These lessons have stood my in good stead ever since. And they kindled in me a desire to *win*.

TWO YEARS LATER, AS A COLLEGE STUDENT at the University of Chicago, my friend Peter led me to the student newspaper, the *Maroon*. I became a sub-editor and reporter, and thereby began developing the skills needed for newspaper work. The big deal at the *Maroon*, however, was that it was controlled by a group of young communists who met secretly elsewhere —"The Maroon Group." It pretty much determined what was to be covered, how, and by whom. They skewed Left. It was a classic example of how communists could control a left-leaning but non-communist organization. I joined this group and participated in its subversive endeavor. This of course turned the staff's democratic decision-making into a charade.

I advanced to become the paper's business manager. But my parents' insistence that I go elsewhere to finish college meant that I had to leave the University of Chicago and the *Maroon* after two years — too soon to qualify as editor. But as I left, one member of our group made a lanyard for me to carry the key to the office of the student paper at the school I was transferring to, Brandeis University.

The paper there was called *The Justice*, which I joined. The skills I had brought from Chicago, and my abilities and enjoyment of the work, led me to be elected editor two years later.

How did my left-wing aspirations fare at Brandeis? Not well! Without comrades to bolster them, as at the *Maroon*, they fell away. My first *Justice* editorial was a tribute to Ferdinand the Bull, as in the children's story: I reproached my fellow students for picking flowers and trampling the school's gardens! I was not exactly preaching Revolution. Indeed the idea of the proletariat state had lost what little attraction it ever had had. Rather it was opposition to the present state of affairs that held my attraction. I wanted to destroy — overturn — authority. This was my pleasure. This was my goal: Destroy the real world that had crippled me as a misfit! *That's* what I wanted to do.

It came to me, however, that if I wanted to lead this revolution, I had to be ready to be the leader. Taken to the extreme, I had to be prepared for prison or for death, like the brave heroes of he Abraham Lincoln Brigade in the Spanish Civil War. I wasn't.

This convinced me that I was not a revolutionary leader. I was a frightened young man seeking a place — perhaps a leadership place — in a politically and ideologically chaotic world. I would therefore step back and focus on my more immediate concerns. Later, when I applied for work at the *New York Times*, I was rejected as a writer and as copy boy, which was the lowest line on the city room manifest, the guy who was sent out to the delicatessen for coffee. I was hired for the same job across town, at the *New York Daily News*.

When I was older, and a freelance writer, I joined the Society of Magazine Writers, now the American Society of Journalists and Authors (ASJA). I participated in the work of running the organization, and this soon earned me its presidency. A few years later, I joined the National Association of Science Writers (NASW). This was then an outfit by and for science journalists from the major daily newspapers. They succeeded each other as presidents with uncontested annual elections.

Again, I found myself working for the group, and reached the point where there was no other likely candidate for the next year's presidency. So I decided to stand for the office. I made an agreement with the vice presidential candidate that we would not oppose, but would support, each other.

Now, however, my lack of newspapers credentials came to the fore. The Old Guard newspaper people caucused. One of them, Phil Boffey, a science writer at the *New York Times*, challenged me. Boffey had not been very active in running the organization, as far as I could see. I had never seen him performing any of the housekeeping work required to keep a professional organization up and running. But this was now that rare thing in NASW, a competitive election.

I thought my chances were good nonetheless. But shortly before the vote, the vice presidential candidate, Joann Rodgers of the *Baltimore American*, reneged on our agreement. She sent a post card to every member saying so, in effect urging them to vote for Boffey.

It was heart-breakingly close. But he beat me 154 to 152.

My loss was painful. But, as I came to realize, it also was a watershed in my career: I had failed to win entrance to the "in" group in my profession, and so I lost the perquisites that such membership provides. The NASW president is of course at the top of the list for conference invitations, plum assignments, and the all important heads-up phone calls on forthcoming news events. He or she is invited to cocktail parties and other occasions to meet and greet important scientists and politicians.

For advancement in journalism, being in the top mix provides contacts and tips that are hard to get if you are out in the cold, especially as a freelance writer sitting home at your desk rather than a staffer who is sought after and courted by the ubiquitous publicity agents in the medical–science–government nexus. I have never regained the access that I might have had if I had won three more votes from my NASW colleagues. To the best of my knowledge, NASW has not had another contested presidential election since then. Clearly, my outsider status was held against me!

The episode taught me something about myself: I was in ongoing conflict *within* myself. On the one hand, as my efforts in NASW showed, I wanted to be "in," to be a winner, to be acknowledged — and accepted — as one of the leaders. As a Number One guy. On the other hand, as my life history clearly showed, I was opposed to the system, to the existing ways and means. I wanted to blow them up. I was a revolutionary. My aim was to destroy the existing order and its truths. This was — is — a no-win situation, and I have not won!

The default position has been to try to convince the mainstream of the wrong-headedness of its views and the correctness of my own extreme positions. My aim is to challenge and confound the status quo with new and better news. And that, I believe, is what a newsman is supposed to do! "The existing order is a lie. Let me tell you the new truth I have discovered!"

One of my first such discoveries involved the NASW itself. This was the time when the scientific case against cigarette smoking had finally won wide public and governmental support. Efforts to challenge the tobacco industry's claim that smoking was harmless were being strongly contested on the basis of huge scientific studies. It struck me as strange, therefore, that at NASW scientific briefings, little was being said about this important development.

Looking around, it became clear why: Big tobacco had placed a spy, an *agent provocateur*, at the nexus of science and the press. In NASW! His name was Leonard Zahn.

He was a sometime journalist who claimed membership in the science-writing club as the representative of the Council for Tobacco Research. This benign sounding organization was created and run by the tobacco industry, specifically to muddy the waters about smoking and illness.

Zahn was a glad-hander. He befriended widely published science writers and hung around with them in science pressrooms. At conferences, he played poker in the evenings with the group's leaders. By day, he worked to keep news of tobacco's dangers out of the papers.

Where could I tell this story? At that time the behind-the-scenes interactions of reporters and those who sought to sway them were not considered to be publishable news. So I wrote up what I discovered, and submitted to the *NASW Newsletter*, which did.

Zahn faded into the woodwork.

8

BRANDEIS

IN THE FALL OF 1952, I WENT TO BRANDEIS UNIVERSITY
in Waltham, Massachusetts, a suburb of Boston. I entered college there as a transfer student, a sophomore. I
was assigned to a men's dorm — where I found new danger:

Each male resident changed his bed linen once a week.
You did this by bringing your soiled sheets to a student
worker, who handled the laundry as part of his athletic
scholarship chores. Complicating matters, this man was a
football player, in fact, the quarterback. I was anti-football,
per my time at the football-free University of Chicago. (The
chancellor there, Robert Hutchins, had banned it years earlier as being inappropriate at a school of higher education.
A controversial decision, but one the UC had stuck to.
Only after Hutchins left did intercollegiate football make a
comeback there.)

The sheets I returned showed signs of urine if you looked at them closely. The quarterback didn't. I tossed them into the pile, and, relieved, left with a fresh set. But it was clear to me that if I continued what I had been doing all my life, sooner or later I would be found out — and would be shamed all over the campus.

Fortunately! Fortunately! My fear of discovery and humiliation appeared to reach whatever part of my soul was responsible for my enuresis. Because, at that moment, it stopped!

The next night and the next week, I was dry, and the next and the next! There may have been one or two relapses, but this dreadful symptom suddenly stopped!

Clearly, my unconscious had reacted to fear. But, as I thought about it, Was this the way most children dried up? I doubted that. Still do. In "normal" boys and girls, is it fear or shame that spurs this developmental advance? My development clearly was different, and I could not discover why I had stopped.

I found, much later, that bed-wetting may have been exacerbated by my mother. She writes in an entry in my Baby Book dated May 1937, when I was almost three, that belladonna, an antispasmodic, was prescribed "in the hope it would help in training for bed wetting." She adds: "It only made matters worse."

I wonder what that "training" was about at age three. Could *it* have made matters worse?

My main activity at Brandeis, other than schoolwork, was the campus newspaper, the *Justice*. I intended to be Editor.

There was no left-wing group controlling the *Justice*; indeed there was only one other far-leftist like myself on campus, and she had other rows to hoe. My fellow staff members were mostly apolitical. They were also less well versed in newspaper work than I was. So my effort was to develop my own and their journalistic skills. When the time came, they elected me editor, albeit there was opposition from my predecessor, who thought I was too radical.

My major political dust-up came when the film club announced that they were going to show *The Birth of a Nation*, David Ward Griffith's 1915 salute to the Confederacy and the Civil War South. The film is strongly racist. In it, black people are depicted as animals. It is also a landmark in film history because of its technical innovations.

I had already seen the film. But carrying my University of Chicago experience over to Brandeis, I strongly opposed showing it there. My reason, which was partially concocted, was that it would insult Brandeis's few black students (and fewer faculty members) to show it.

My classmate Mel Nash and I took our opposition to the showing to a meeting of the Student Council, which was sponsoring the film. If it must be screened, we said, it should be accompanied by an expert panel that would put it in context. A fellow student, Gene Pugatch, argued the other side, and said that to ban it would be censorship.

My classmate, John Howard, rose to describe the lynchings and riots that had followed some showings of the film. He added that, as a black man, he would be personally hurt and troubled if *Birth of a Nation* were shown. Another student, Harry Morrison, stood to say that since *I, David*, had seen the film, he felt that he should be able to do so as well. He urged it be shown. Watching it, he said, would prepare student viewers for the prejudice they would see in their own lives.

The question was called on a motion that the film not be shown the following Sunday. The motion was voted down. A new motion was proposed, that the film be shown along with a faculty–student panel. Pugatch attacked this idea as "subtle censorship." But when the vote came, it passed almost unanimously.

Meanwhile, the Boston NAACP and the Boston Jewish Community issued statements against the showing. The student council met again, for four hours, and again reversed its position: *Don't show it.*

The student body quickly jumped into the fray, voting first to show the film and then, in a tense assembly, voting not to.

I was called out for my hypocrisy — I had seen it, but others shouldn't — and rightly so. Nevertheless, I saw the "Don't show it!" vote as a victory — though I regret it today.

The resolution of this conflict depends in part on *how* a hateful film is shown, and to whom. I believe in free expression. But do you hurt people with it? Would Brandeis show the pro-Nazi film *The Way of the World* on its Jewish campus? I think not. It, like *Birth of a Nation*, is perhaps more acceptable if couched as "cinema studies" rather than as entertainment.

One might wonder what, besides photography, newspapering, and student politics I was doing about the reason I had come to college, i.e., studies. Brandeis had a stunning faculty made up in part of European Jewish immigrants, escapees from Hitler. I relished the work with them but failed to excel as I had hoped to. This was brought home to me just prior to graduation.

The time had come for the faculty to honor students' academic achievements by assigning honors, based on grades. My grade point average was not too bad — it was about a high B. But it was not in the As. I could not hope for highest honors (*summa cum laude*), which would have required most, if not all, As. I hoped for high honors (*magna cum laude*), but just then a C+ came in. *Magna* was out! I was distraught. It is true that I had not established myself in any academic discipline. My A.B. degree would be in History and English. But I had not immersed myself in either one, or any other. *Cum laude* was the best I could get!

I was devastated, shamed, humiliated. My parents were

coming to graduation. I phoned, asking that they not come. No chance of that! They'd bought their train tickets. I wanted to skip graduation. But that was no longer an option. I was sick with shame: a failure.

They didn't rub it in.

It rained during commencement.

9

ABROAD

I WAS AT LOOSE ENDS IN CHICAGO. I missed Brandeis. My father, Zim, stepped in with a generous promise; he'd finance a year of study abroad!

I sailed for France on the *SS Flandre*. Ostensibly, I would study philosophy at the Sorbonne in Paris. But in reality, I was focused on solving my big problem, my fear of women and of sex. I was disinterested in laying the ground work for a career or profession, which my Brandeis classmates were all doing. When I solve my problem, I told myself, then my life will *begin*. I was twenty years old, and *far* off pace.

But the Sorbonne was out of reach. My French was not good enough for me to fill out the registration forms. When I did finally get to class, there was no class!

Instead there was riot. The students were on strike and

fighting each other over issues I little understood. They were in the courtyards, fighting each other and the police, who'd been sent to restore order. I abandoned the Sorbonne and registered instead at the language school, the *Alliance Française*, where I did improve my French.

I had no friends.

I had grown bored with essentially doing nothing.

I hitchhiked south to Marseille. A shabby passenger ship, the *Negbah,* was docked there. It was en route to the far eastern end of the Mediterranean, to Israel. Might I do better there? I bought a cheap passage, and got aboard. Who I was — my life — seemed to change.

I was a Sunday School Jew, and not a religious one. I had no sense that I lived in a universe overseen by god. I still don't. But the *Negbah* was filled with Jews who did. Refugees from the Holocaust, and from post-war Europe, they were bound for a home that they, like me, had never seen.

The ship stopped at Naples, time enough for me to visit Pompei. But I had another goal in Italy: I had been told that I could buy there a special kind of pocket knife. Most switchblade knives open visibly from the handle, in a circular path. The type I sought, illegal in Italy and elsewhere, opened straight out of the end of the handle, impelled by a powerful spring. You could lean up against a person, press the handle, and spring the blade forward so that it invisibly stabbed through the person's clothing into his or her body without ever being seen. Fortunately, I say now in retrospect, I could not find a swithblade — and we sailed out of the Bay of Naples without one.

Most of my shipmates were older, tired, men and women — Jews I had not personally encountered. Our conversations changed my sense of who I was, *not* a Sunday School Jew any more, but now simply a Jew, an historical Jew like the others.

It took the *Negbah* several more days to reach Israeli waters. It was well after midnight when the lights of Haifa rose into view. Everyone was awake and on deck. I don't recall if they sang "Hatikvah," but they certainly cheered their arrival home. I was deeply moved.

During the next two months I visited and worked on two kibbutzes: Gesher HaZiv in Galilee, and Nirim south of Tel Aviv on the edge of the Gaza strip; the lights of Khan Yunis were visible out the window.

The work I enjoyed most was bringing hay in from the fields. I would stick a hay bale with a pitchfork, swing it up and overhead to a farmer standing high on the hay rick above me. I was pleased to learn this maneuver, and I was pleased, too, to have the strength to perform it. I also worked in the sugar beet field — work I enjoyed.

Because it was so close to the border, Nirim had a detachment of young soldiers from the Israeli Defense Force (IDF) in residence. I became friends with an UZI-toting young woman soldier. She was a Yemenite, and we got along quite well despite the fact that we couldn't speak each other's language. I liked the feeling of hanging out with a tough but sweet military woman. About the only thing I could say in Hebrew when I searched her out at the end of the work day was "*Efo Teertza?*" Where is Tertsa? These are the words I can still recall sixty years later.

Unlike my shipmates on the *Negbah*, I was not scouting out an iminent move to Israel. I was very curious but not committed to changing my life in that way. After a couple of months, I had had enough, and I headed back to Paris. I was trying to solve a problem, not remake my life. But I wasn't making much progress.

Several months later I overcame my fear one spring evening. I went to a neighborhood on the Right Bank where I was not known. I feared being shamed in Montparnasse, my usual stomping grounds.

The trees that lined the boulevards there were in bloom. I walked for a while, then stepped into a restaurant for dinner. Then, more wandering. It was getting dark, and I felt it was getting too late — for what? Finally, breaking through my conflict, I entered a bar at street level that I knew was a whorehouse.

I ordered a drink. Soon, a woman — an older woman — sat down next to me.

Did I want to go upstairs? I didn't — but I did. I had trapped myself. I had to agree or leave. Fearfully, I said yes. I agreed to her price and paid her. We got off our bar stools, and she led the way to a carpeted staircase at the front of the bar. We started up.

At the moment we reached the first landing, I suddenly had a strong visual image: my mother's face. This was the only time before or since I have seen her in this way. I do not remember whether her face was superimposed on the woman I was with or, rather, an apparition in the air. But it was unmistakably my mother's.

Was it a sign to retreat downstairs, or an indication to go forward? Having come this far, I wasn't going to retreat.

We entered a room with a bed. She pulled off her skirt, and lay down. I undressed. I came to her, hugged her. I slid in beside her. "No kisses!" she said. I tried to find a hard-on. Couldn't. I climbed on top of her, and pressed her with my hips. No feeling! Nothing was happening. I stayed that way until I was exhausted. Nothing happened. I had no erotic feelings, no erection. Nothing.

Stalling for time, I asked her to stay the night with me. She said no, she couldn't. She lived in a suburb and had to catch the Metro home. She was not angry or upset. But I was devastated. I got off the bed. Dressed. Said thank you! And left.

I was proud to have overcome my terror, and gotten that far. But I quickly realized that I had failed again.

Shortly thereafter, I took the boat train to La Havre, and embarked for home.

10

PSYCHOANALYSIS

I ARRIVED BACK IN NEW YORK from a year in Europe and Israel sick and upset. I phoned my girlfriend, Susan Berlin, and asked her to meet me in a bar. Her mother refused to let her meet me there.

In a confused and chaotic week, I was told that I needed professional help. Inwardly fearful, I visited a psychologist. He agreed: I needed treatment.

A quick trip to Chicago — where my father's experts concurred. He would defray the cost, as I had neither income nor a job. Back in New York, I was referred to Dr. Emanuel Peterfreund — a psychoanalyst. He told me when I went to meet him at his office in the 90s on the East Side that "this will be the hardest thing you ever do. And it will take a long time." He was right on both counts.

I knew very little about psychiatric treatment. In college

I'd read a few essays by Sigmund Freud. But they said little about the psychiatric process that I now was entering.

Movies about psychoanalysis fail to depict what is happening, because there is little to depict visually: a patient lying on his or her back on a couch; an analyst seated out of view, behind him or her. But as I discovered, much *is* going on. The patient, energized by the analyst's presence, has begun to say, sing, or shriek whatever is in his or her head, trying to get out.

All of our heads are filled with a usually silent mélange of thoughts and feelings. And if the patient is mentally ill, which is the reason to be lying there in the first place, these concerns and emotions likely will be expressed sooner or later.

This talking — emoting — is like a river. It starts small. But through months and then years it grows in size and in force. A rivulet becomes a stream and then a torrent. And what is spun away in the flow are a lifetime of feelings and thoughts that have been repressed, hidden from consciousness — where they now appear and can be heard. Hidden anger and pain appear; remembering them and expressing them is painful — in some instances quite painful.

In this process, the outside of the mind (*ego*) eats away its memories and falls back in time. It eventually returns one to one's childhood. In a frighteningly real sense, during the psychoanalytic hour the patient is returned to his or her childhood. If there had been major emotional disruptions (trauma) that have remained hidden and have disrupted the patient's later life, they may be exposed, and can be discussed and understood by the analyst and the patient. These behaviors thus can be partly defanged.

All this takes time, much time: In my extraordinarily long case, some fourteen years. A long, long time, during which my focus of attention was myself, my analysis, to the detriment of current interests, such as work — which suffered as the result.

In those years I discovered my mother's dislike for me, and the damage this had done to my self-confidence and my sexuality. I also rediscovered Snookie, the cloth animal, a toy that apparently had become my life partner in feeling, in the absence of much feeling for or about my mother.

This was a truly surprising rediscovery! Away from my analyst's office, away from him, I formulated in my mind a children's story — the only one I have ever thought to write.

I conjured up an animal, a unique and wonderful one. A friendly animal who lived in the wonderful palace garden of an oriental prince. This small animal was unique. He spoke English, for one thing. He was friendly for another. And for a third thing, he had not one furry tail. He had two. Two tails. One for him, and one, of course, for me!

These incidents and my recall of them here provided me with a sense of the power of my analysis. This process is commonly described as a "conversation" between analyst and patient. It may commence that way, but once the method hits its stride it has become a rushing, headlong force, a rebel freight train made up of language and groans, cries and other sounds, a whirlwind of sound, fear, pain that is triggered by the analyst's presence. Despite this, there is the hope that the whirlwind will expend itself, and a better feeling, a state of security, of health, will replace it.

Psychoanalysis was relatively inexpensive then. It cost me $15.00 per hour, five hours a week. This was roughly my weekly salary at the *Daily News* and later at *The New York Post*. Fortunately, my father recognized my need, and paid for most of it.

Much later, after he died, it turned out that my mother had kept track of all these reimbursements. My dad had left me a good bit of money; she was his executor.

When she wrote me a check, she appended a note, saying that she had *deducted* from the total the amount that he had sent me through the years. (In the scheme of things, as inflation mounted, this was not a big deal.)

Sally blamed my treatment, along with the Reds I had associated with at the University of Chicago, for all that was wrong with me. "If you'd listened to me, I would have told you what to do!" she said. But I didn't listen then; and I now remain curious about what she thought I ought have done with my life. It could not have been pleasant.

I I

RH

I ANSWERED A CLASSIFIED AD and was hired for my first full-time writing job. It was at a medical news magazine, *Medical World News.* The job required two things I had learned in journalism: an ability to do tabloid writing, and an understanding of medicine — which in these days was *much* simpler than it has become today. It was not long before I was catching critical assignments, like covering scientific reports at the annual convention of the American Medical Association (AMA).

One development close to home, at the Columbia University Medical College, particularly caught my eye: Two young researchers there, Drs. John Gorman, a pathologist, and an obstetrician Vincent Freda, were developing a treatment to prevent Rh disease of newborn babies. This fairly common lethal disease occurs after a woman, blood type

Rh negative, delivers a baby that carries its father's Rh positive blood type.

Gorman and Freda decided that the disease occurs when an Rh negative mother delivers her first Rh positive fetus. A small amount of fetal blood, perhaps a teaspoonful or less, crosses into her circulation, triggering her immune system to attack Rh positive blood. This is likely to happen the next time she becomes pregnant with an Rh positive fetus: This mother now attacks her fetus's Rh positive blood, sickening and often killing it. This rarely happens during a woman's first Rh incompatible pregnancy. But once it does occur, the disease gets worse on each successive pregnancy, so eventually she may lose a half dozen or more offspring.

The two researchers were testing this hypothesis by injecting Rh negative prisoners at New York's Sing Sing prison with Rh positive blood. The men, like Rh negative pregnant women, became sensitized to Rh positive blood that, by definition, carried the Rh factor. But when given the Rh negative injections derived from the serum, the clear portion of blood, of Rh negative individuals, they did *not* become sensitized. As men, they were of course at no risk of Rh disease.

This struck me as very provocative work! I quit my job in order to write a book about it. The science grew more complicated, in part because another group of researchers, in Liverpool, England, using different scientific clues had — simultaneously — come to the same conclusion: an Rh positive bleed by a fetus into an Rh negative mother triggered this disease. And both Liverpool and New York had come to the same hypothesis: If the Rh positive blood could be neutralized, Rh disease would be forestalled. It wouldn't happen.

To write this story, I visited Sing Sing and interviewed officials there. More important, I visited — often — Gorman and Freda at Columbia. They were generously willing to explain their work, and, what was more, explain the biology and what they surmised was the pathology of Rh disease.

Both teams came up with the surprising, and risky-sounding, proposal that the way to prevent the mother from becoming sensitized to the Rh factor was to inject her, right after her Rh incompatible delivery, with anti Rh antibody, so as to destroy any Rh positive blood cells that had leaked into her circulation.

This treatment worked: Rh negative women injected with Rh positive antibody at delivery of an Rh positive baby did not become sensitized to the Rh factor, and their next Rh positive fetus was spared the disease. This treatment worked virtually every time, opening the way for doctors to eliminate the scourge. Strangely, both New York and Liverpool advanced ideas on how and why this method works. Both ideas have been found to be wrong. No one today knows why this treatment works. But it does! Tens of thousands of babies have been spared illness and death in the fifty years since this treatment became commercially available.

Confusing matters, the Americans and the British have different nomenclatures for describing this work, as follows:

U.S.	Britain
Rh	D
Rh negative	D negative
Rh positive	D positive
Rh factor	D

I visited Liverpool to interview the researchers there. Neither I nor my wife, Veva, had been there before. I brought her along — and we met some unpleasant surprises.

Veva was black. The chief of the Liverpool team, Sir Cyril A. Clarke, and his wife Féo, were Establishment white. They invited us for tea. It was a stiff encounter, and as the days went by it grew hostile. The doctor who had done the key discovery work, Dr. Ronald Finn, it turned out, was Jewish. I of course planned to credit him for it.

This angered Sir Cyril when he found out. He tried to steal Finn's credit by saying that the key insight came to his wife in a dream one night while she was asleep. When I indicated that I believe Finn, and would say so, he told me he had connections in London, and that, if I credited Finn, my book would never be published in Great Britain.

It never has!

My book, *Rh, The Intimate History of a Disease and*

Its Conquest, was published in New York by Macmillan in the spring of 1973. All but one of the reviews were good. But the one I wanted — needed the most — one from the *New York Times Book Review* — never occurred.

I hired a PR firm, and they got me time on a lot of lesser TV and radio stations — but none seemed to sell books. Then, in August, the daily *Times* published a book review by a science editor and writer there, who had just happened to spot *Rh* on a table in the book review office — and was ecstatic as he read it. I was ecstatic at what he wrote:

> *Zimmerman's book tells the fascinating story of this medical advance, progress that now routinely saves the lives of thousands of babies. . .who would have died if born even 25 years ago. . . .Mr. Zimmerman an able—and on the evidence of this book, extraordinarily industrious science writer. . .tells the complex story as clearly as possible. . . .[He] has given here a classic account that skillfully exploits all the ironies involved. . . . Mr. Zimmerman's tale is perhaps most valuable as an account of how scientific advance is really made. . . . The reality with Rh disease was [that] progress was often a matter of accident and blind luck, of coincidences that no one could have foreseen or planned... This is a very interesting book deserving of a wide audience—not least among those who make policy in matters of*

medical research as well as among those interested in the reality of scientific discovery rather than its mythology.

You simply could not ask for a better book review! The word was getting around! In early December, in time for Christmas, I had *two* segments with Barbara Walters on *The Today Show.*

What more could an author ask for!

But there was no boost in sales. Later I found out why. There were very few *Rh* books in the stores, no more than 5,000 copies coast-to-coast. Not enough to create any excitement whatsoever.

There was nothing more I could do.

Vince Freda has died. So has Ronnie Finn. On trips to Liverpool, I have worked with his widow, Joan, to overcome British agents' and publishers' reluctance, but we failed. *Rh* fell from sight in New York and never appeared in London.

And then!

The year 2018 was the fiftieth anniversary of the vaccine's commercial approval. It has been an enormous medical success. There has been one change: *RhoGAM* was developed by Ortho Diagnostics, a division of Johnson & Johnson in Oradell, New Jersey. But in 2014 Ortho sold the rights to it to Kedrion Biopharma, Inc., an international company headquartered in Barga, Italy. More important for me, Kedrion planned a conference in New York to mark RhoGAM's fiftieth anniversary. Their representative here, Richard Hendrick, asked; would I take part?

I said Yes!

Hendrick had found me through *Rh*. He told me he wanted me to speak at this conference, which would be held at Columbia, where John Gorman and Vince Freda had conducted their research.

I went with Hendrick to a planning meeting at Columbia. At one moment there were four people in an office: me, and three Rh experts, *all* of whom had read my book! I was in heaven; my expertise was *finally* acknowledged by these experts!

It turned out that I was *the* expert on the early events. No one else had written a book on them, and most of the participants had died. John Gorman, now living in California, and I were the only survivors, along with Dr. Alvin Zipursky in Canada. I experienced the thrill that professional historians must enjoy, as being sole pathfinders to an important past.

What is more, and rare for a book on medicine or science, what I captured a half century ago remains valid and true. Few science writers have been so fortunate. I am deeply hopeful that my book will be republished in the U.S., and that a way now can be found to publish a first British edition in London!

12

SHERRY AND JUDY

THE ARRIVAL OF FIDEL CASTRO'S REVOLUTIONARIES in Havana in the late '50s, and their seizure of power in Cuba, created great excitement in the U.S. Americans took sides: pro or con the Cuban revolution. I, needless to say, was pro. But, most of all, I opposed the call for an American invasion to put Castro down.

I decided to visit the island to see things for myself. I booked a flight via the Fair Play for Cuba organization, and in the summer of 1960, I flew to Havana.

With only very rudimentary Spanish and little sense of the political dynamics, I went to mass rallies and visited government agencies. I learned slogans of the Revolution. For example: *Si las causas de Fidel son las causas comunistas, agrégame a la lista. Estoy de acuerdo con él* (if the causes of Fidel are communist causes, then add me to the list. I am in agreement with him!). I interviewed Fidelistas and befriended a politically connected Habanera who assured me that Castro was not torturing or shooting his adversaries. He took me on a late-night tour of the City's main prison to prove this to me. It didn't.

The pre-Castro amenities still existed in Havana, including the grandiose hotels built for American gamblers and tourists of the previous regime. So in the afternoons I would go to the roof of one of these hotels, where there was a huge, elegant swimming pool. I would dive in and swim some laps.

One day I swam to the far end of the pool, surfaced, and looked up— and there was a Brandeis schoolmate, Judy Gorbach, looking down at me! Surprise! We were delighted to see one another and that evening she and her husband, Sherry (Sherwood), and I met for dinner.

At Brandeis, Judy had danced and studied sociology. Sherry had been a dormmate with whom I had worked on several left-wing causes. They since had wed.

Sherry had been headed for a career at his father's insurance business in Connecticut. But, he told me, it did not appeal to him. He quit. He went back to school as a pre-med student and earned his M.D. Now he was a resident at the Tufts New England Medical Center. He and Judy had spent the summer at a public health project in Guatemala. On their way home, they stopped off in Cuba to see its revolution, particularly its progress in improving medical care and public health.

Over dinner, Sherry told me that he and Judy planned to drive a rental car to Santiago de Cuba at the far east end of the island (adjacent to the U.S.-controlled Guantanamo Bay U.S. naval installation). Would I like to join them?

You bet I would!

And I was grateful to learn that Sherry spoke fluent Spanish and could converse with the Cuban doctors and officials we met along the way in our week of travel.

The officials we met were young Fidelistas sent from Havana to deliver health care to Cuba's rural poor (*campesinos*). Sherry's experience — and expertise — in facing similar medical and sanitation problems in Latin America made us welcome guests at facilities along the way.

When I returned to New York, I transformed my notes of these encounters into a manuscript for a book. I reported what I had seen and heard. But I was careful not to shade my report to either the pro- or anti-Castro side. I felt that a reportorial, non-judgmental stance, however thin my knowledge and understanding of the inflammatory political situation, would be the only way I could contribute to the public debate. My manuscript was brief, about one hundred or so typescript pages. But when it was finished, I could not find anyone who wanted to publish it. What is more, the separation and conflict between the two sides had progressed so rapidly that my take on conditions in August was superseded by hostile events in December.

My manuscript never was published, and unfortunately I lost it as I moved from place to place in subsequent months.

What didn't get lost was my friendship with Sherry and Judy! We often spoke by phone, and I visited them in Boston, where Sherry was completing his medical internship in infectious diseases at Tufts. Soon they moved to Queens, in New York City, so Sherry could pursue a residency at Bellevue Hospital in Manhattan.

Going to their home for a weekend overnight visit was for me to enter a different, wonderful world from the grim place I was living, on the top floor of a six-floor walkup on West 104th Street. Their first daughter, Roxanne, named after the heroine in the play *Cyrano de Bergerac*, had joined the grown-up household, and on Sunday mornings we sat around noshing on whitefish and lox and bagels. To me it was a scene of domestic tranquility such as I'd never before experienced. Then, in the evenings, I'd ride the subway back to Manhattan to my home, where rats had been playing in my absence. (One rat had gotten into a pound package of sliced bread, and had carried it, one slice at a time, down to her nest in the basement.)

My psychoanalysis meanwhile was becoming more difficult, more painful, and more frightening. I was out of touch, crazy. This came to a head near Christmas, when I experienced terrifying emotional changes. I was incoherent in my daily sessions. I experienced out-of-body feelings.

My personality, my soul it seemed, disintegrated. I was in hell, with no place to go or to hide.

One session was so tumultuous that I could not walk out of the doctor's office. I could not get home.

Panicked, I phoned the Gorbachs and told them of my acute distress. As if by a miracle, Sherry agreed to come and pick me up. Gratefully, I waited in the lobby until he came. I got into the car, and he drove us to his home in Queens. Refuge! When I looked at myself in the mirror, my eyes were wide with fear.

I slept on the couch that night. The next day, Sherry or Judy drove me back to my doctor's office and waited until I emerged to carry me back to their home. I told the doctor that I was crazed — I didn't know how I could carry on. "With what is happening," he told me, "I can help you *much* more!"

As I came to understand it, what had happened was that, by talking and carrying on over the years, I had re-gressed, talked my way back, so that my soul (*id*) had pulled apart from my everyday self (*ego*). Now I could look ob-jectively at my id. I could now analyze *myself*. But it was weeks, months, before I could live and function with those foundational changes. Meanwhile, the Gorbachs kindly kept me. I spent the days running suburban errands with Judy and Roxanne.

During this period, Sherry one night brought home to dinner a medical school classmate, a psychiatrist in training, who was serving an internship at a hospital in the Bronx. She was black, one of the few then in training in New York City hospitals. We didn't talk very much; I was in my bag, and she may have been in hers. She did tell me her name, Veva, and revealed that she had come east from St. Louis to study medicine. Her father was a surgeon, like mine, with a private practice, a wife, a brother and sister, and a home in the suburbs. I had no notion of what we would soon become together.

As time went by, I regained my mind and my health. I needed to stop imposing on the Gorbachs and return home. But I couldn't go back to rats. Veva also needed a new home.

She was due to start a psychiatric residency at Bellevue Hospital and needed to move out of the Bronx, where she had served her internship. One day I said I was going house hunting. She asked if she could come with me. Of course!

Black people were not exactly welcomed in rentals in the better precincts of Manhattan. But we set out together, and headed for the Upper West Side.

We were in luck. We quickly found a *For Rent* sign in the front window of a large ground floor apartment on West 111th Street, a few blocks from Columbia University. To sidestep the racial issue, I went alone to see the agent — and he gave me the lease. All of a sudden, from being two individuals searching for two apartments, we were two individuals renting an apartment together. At the time, I felt that it just sort of happened that way. In retrospect, it strikes me as a case of feminine guile! At any rate, it was a piece of good fortune. Veva and I lived in the eight-flat building for many years. We were wed there and started our family; 603 West 111th Street, with Veva, was a place of much comfort and relief.

13

VEVA

VEVA WAS THE BEST THING — the *best person* — who ever entered my life. It is hard to say how influential she has been to me, to my life.

She loved me! I loved her!

She was loving. Much of the time, I was mean, stewing in my poor sexual performance, rejecting her, and dreaming of my great sexual triumphs when psychoanalysis delivered me into a realm of full sexual conquest — which of course never happened.

I did successfully impregnate her. Finally she put it all on the line: If I would not marry her, then she was going to leave. Crudely, I reasoned with myself: A bird in the hand was worth more than two in the bush. I asked her to marry me. She accepted.

Despite my reticence, the planning and preparation for

the wedding was an exhilarating time. My rabbi from Chicago, the one who had had me read *Joseph in Egypt*, was going to be in New York for a meeting. So we scheduled the wedding for that period, after he agreed to officiate. Robena came from Chicago, as did Veva's folks from St. Louis. My dad, Zim, was going to be at a medical convention in Seattle but managed to fly in. My mother, having learned to her dismay that Veva was *not* a Hebrew name, wasn't invited, and wouldn't have come if she had been . . . .

Now, I am a white man. And Veva was a black woman. This was not a common coupling in the mid-1950s. But it concerned those who knew us far more than it concerned us. It didn't! (The *New York Times* published a wedding announcement with Veva's photo.) Ceremonies over, the party was in full swing. We took a helicopter to JFK airport and an overnight flight to St. Thomas for our honeymoon.

Despite the different colors of our skins, we were very much alike, as were our families. With no prompting, my father, Zim, a surgeon, had recently written to Veva's dad, Henry, congratulating him on his election to the American College of Surgeons, a prestigious organization.

At our level, Veva had far more prestige than I did. She had graduated from Wellesley College, had earned her M.D., and would serve her residency in psychiatry at the legendary Bellevue Hospital in Manhattan.

Veva grew up just before the Civil Rights Era. Her aims were professional service. But her younger siblings, Henry and Judy Hampton, matured in that era and devoted their lives to civil rights. Their father, of an earlier age, had made it his business as a leading black doctor to create relationships with the dominant white power structure. He built a large surgical and medical practice downtown, where, unfortunately, he also had a drug store. Narcotics were sold there, and Dr. Hampton began using the easily available Demerol and developed a drug habit. His mind and his health deteriorated as the result. He never recovered.

Veva had inherited her dad's respect for medical institutions and her family's rejection of racial segregation. She and her siblings, for example, were forbidden to attend segregated movies and other segregated events. They were raised oblivious to racism, which her family believed was on the way out. Years later, while already a practicing psychiatrist in New York, Veva phoned me one afternoon in tears: She had been Jim Crowed verbally in a store in a Manhattan — and I left my job ASAP to hold and comfort her.

It's worth noting that Veva reached maturity a year or so before the Civil Rights Era, and focused on professional obligations and rewards. Her sister and brother, a couple of years younger, grew up in the midst of the Movement. Veva and I fortunately suffered very few racial attacks. Fortunately, too, while I was the principal breadwinner at first, her starting salary at New York University, which administered Bellevue, and her fees from the private psychiatric practice that she conducted out of an office on East 87th Street at Madison Avenue, made her our top earner, cushioning my highs and lows as a freelance writer. She worked well within the strictures of NYU's Department of Psychiatry.

But Veva's attraction did not relate to her titles and skills. Rather, it was her personality — her *sparkling* personality — that drew people, her family, patients, colleagues, strangers to her.

She made you happy to be with her. That was the influence that she had on me, and I believe most others who met her. She got along with all sorts.

In the late '90s, Veva bought a brownstone house in a nice neighborhood. We couldn't afford it. She decided to rent one floor and bought a *For Rent* ad. Soon two women showed up and agreed to her stiff monthly price. They left, and then returned with a paper bag filled with small bills. More than $10,000.

"Veva. Do you know what you're doing?" people cautioned her. She persevered.

Only after they moved in did it become clear who they were: We now were living with a whorehouse as our downstairs neighbors! The madam was the lady with the cash in a paper bag. She installed some decorative lights by the front door and told us our street was now under surveillance (she didn't say by whom), and so we'd be safer.

Her girls, she told us, were clean and of good character

— they all were college undergraduates from New York University. She and Veva got along well. Veva was, by then, a dean at NYU's Medical School, and she felt obligated to tell her boss, the top dean, what she was into. When she did, she reported, he chuckled, and offered her neighborly advice on living cheek and jowl with "sin."

When Veva was promoted to "Dean Zimmerman," I thought this was a reward for her clinical psychiatric work. But in fact, it represented NYU's effort to create a more broadly representative Dean's Office. Veva was the first woman and the first black person, of course, to work there. This became clear when she discovered that she had little deaning to do. She was a public relations asset for NYU.

So she set her own agenda. Most notably, she created a program in which New York City high school students were brought into the NYU hospitals for lectures, classes, and hands-on work with staff doctors and scientists. This proved so successful in filling an educational need in the public schools that Veva upgraded the program to a New York City high school, the Salk School. She wrote to the polio vaccine pioneer Jonas Salk and asked permission to use his name. He agreed, and the Salk School of Science is now past its twentieth birthday, well received as an example of how a medical school can become an educational opportunity for its neighborhood children. The Salk School of Science is a success — Veva's legacy.

In 2007, Veva and I flew to Iceland and then joined a

shipboard tour to Greenland. There we boarded smaller boats to tour the iceberg-filled waters, and marveled at the exotic seascape they presented.

Then, as we sailed back to Iceland, the ship became caught up in a force-ten Atlantic storm. Up and down on massive waves, we were tied up with ropes to our bunks. There was no way to walk around the ship. We were badly shaken up and seasick, and as the storm abated and we approached the lights of Reykjavíc, Veva still was ill.

She never fully recovered. Doctors back home in Vermont diagnosed her with what I recall was a uterine cancer. I drove her to the University of Vermont Medical Center in Burlington. They refused to treat her: Her cancer was too far along. Panicked, we phoned Sherry Gorbach. He referred us to an oncologist in Boston who was developing potent drug regimens to treat Veva's type of malignancy. We returned there every few weeks; I slept in an apartment in the hospital.

But Veva was dying. She decided that she wanted to die at home, where we had moved in Vermont, two hundred miles to the northeast, out of immediate reach of the hospital.

At this moment our younger son, Tobias, then in his twenties, revealed a bold plan of his own that we had not been aware of. He wanted his mom in the safest possible place. So he had arranged to buy or rent a house near the hospital, and he had taken all the necessary steps for Veva to move in and be cared for in Boston.

It was a bold plan, and we all considered it. Finally, I told Tobey that I was Veva's legal guardian, and I did not see proximity to the hospital as meaningfully helpful in her quest for survival. I said I would take her back to Sheffield, as we had decided. And I did, although she was by now sick enough that the doctor would not allow me to drive her in the car. She returned home the last time in an ambulance. Veva died several days later, January 2008, at home. The boys and I were grief stricken. I am sure Tobey was angry with me, and rightfully so. We have never discussed it. I continue to deeply regret our conflict, more than a decade later.

OUR FIRSTBORN SON, JACOB, OR J.B. as he quickly came to be called, was sturdy and self-confident from birth in 1969. By the time he was two, he was conversing on a par with us and other adults.

He was gregarious and particularly loved and admired Veva's brother, Henry Hampton. Henry owned and flew an airplane, drove a sports car, and produced motion pictures as a P.R. Rep of the Universalist Church in Boston — a compelling role model.

J.B. was cute child, no doubt about it. By the time he was five or six, he was taking music lessons — the drums — and quickly became quite good at it. Sadly, he soon dropped this music to pursue other adventures.

Adolescence stymied him, however. He had a few dates but failed to meld into the pre-teen social scene. One particularly visible problem was his size. Like Veva and his Uncle Henry, J.B. was overweight, ashamed, and grew shy. And socially isolated, albeit he made and kept many male and female friends, from his high school, Fieldston in the Bronx. He started an annual party at our house in Vermont, and each year thirty or forty of his contemporaries come to our Sheffield house for Baconfest, where they consume huge amounts of beer and bacon over several days, sheltered indoors from the miserable cold of Vermont's winter winds. The party occurs on the celebration of Martin Luther King's Birthday in mid-January.

J.B.'s existential ambivalence at first was expressed by his retreat into his bedroom for much of the celebration. Through the years, however, he has come into his own as host and master of ceremonies at the annual party.

This reflects a major change in his sense of being. J.B., like his mom Veva and his beloved uncle Henry, was chubby at birth and began to grow fat as an adolescent. He was embarrassed and worse, shamed. Psychiatric therapy did not help. Finally, as his weight passed three hundred pounds, he radically changed his life. He chose a surgical approach in which, carefully monitored medically, he allowed his stomach to be radically reduced in size so that it now contains less than a fourth of its original volume. He couldn't hold much food, so he ate far less — a permanent, radically restricted diet — and as the result he lost huge amounts of weight, stabilizing at around two hundred pounds. He could no longer eat carbohydrates, consuming instead miniscule amounts of protein and spirits, which were and are allowed. To match his svelt new shape, J.B. slowly took control of his life in his forties. He began to date again. He met a woman, a Korean American psychotherapist, and they began to go steady. Her name is Gloria. She is lovely.

They were engaged in 2018 and wed in 2019. Sue and I are absolutely delighted!

14

RAPTORS

I WAS WRITING EXCLUSIVELY about medical science in the late 1960s, when I chanced to read a book review in *Science* magazine that turned me in a wholly new direction. The book was the report of a conference of *ornithologists*, bird study scientists, at the University of Wisconsin, in Madison. The topic: the status of America's peregrine falcons (*Falco peregrinus anatum*), also known then as duck hawks.

This falcon had become virtually extinct in the Lower 48 states. As the conference chairman, Joseph Hickey, a leading peregrine biologist, said: "Research on the [U.S.] peregrine population is finished — because there is not much more that can be done for it."

The cause of this catastrophe was known: DDT contamination of the environment, which peregrines imbibed in the song birds upon which they preyed. The pesticide contained a chemical that thinned birds' egg shells, which broke before they hatched, killing the unborn chicks. "The scientists had assembled an irrefutable case," I wrote at the time. "It was too late to be of any value in protecting America's peregrine falcons."

I had never seen a peregrine falcon. But like many birdwatchers, I was upset by this news. More importantly, I was furiously angry at Joseph Hickey. The bird's decline had taken two decades, as he was aware. But as its reigning expert, he appeared to have done nothing to reverse it. He had studied it to its death, without trying to help.

Using his conference report and other scientific material I wrote an impassioned essay describing how scientists, birdwatchers, and the Federal government — a major advocate for spraying DDT — had fiddled while Rome burned. My problem: Who would publish this? A new, counter-cultural magazine, *Scanlons*, had just opened for business. I submitted my essay. They accepted it. But *Scanlons* was going nowhere, and they soon lost interest in my piece. With great trepidation, I went to their office and reclaimed my pages.

Who else would be interested?

Fortunately, one of my colleagues at *Medical Word News* had connections at the *New York Times Magazine*. They were willing to read the piece. I quickly sent it to them.

Eureka!

They loved it. They wanted to publish it! What was more, they wanted a color photo for the magazine's cover. They located an aged peregrine, at a National Audubon Society facility in Boston, and had it photographed. It was a giddy time for me, as they edited the piece — which I had called "Post-Mortem for the Peregrine Falcon." They changed the title to "Death Comes to the Peregrine Falcon" — and they published it, on August 9, 1970.

In my research, I had discovered that not all falcon followers were passive, like Joseph Hickey. Rather, there were people trying to save the bird. Specifically, they were *falconers*, men and women who tamed and used peregrines to hunt for other birds and small mammals. Previously, falconers had robbed young wild peregrines from their nests and trained them to hunt together as a team. They rarely, if ever, tried to breed them in captivity to obtain new hunters. No need to. On the other hand, in training and flying peregrines and other raptors, they learned far more about peregrine biology than anyone else with an interest in the birds.

Now, some of them were eager to create ways to breed the birds for their own use, and to restore the peregrine's devastated wild populations. The leader of this group was the ornithologist and falconer Tom Cade, who was a professor at Cornell University in Ithaca, New York. I visited him there one cold winter day and watched him fly his bird at a practice target, a pigeon tethered to a long cord, that he swung around his head.

The peregrine arose from his wrist, where he carried it, quickly dove down on the training lure. Cade rewarded it with a bit of meat that he kept in a bag tied to his belt.

Tom Cade and the falconers, were reviled as thieves of nature by "dickey birders" (as he called them). They were planning a conservation effort for the peregrine.

IT WAS A JOYOUS MOMENT FOR ME when the *Times* came out with my piece. I had phone calls of congratulation. My boss at the *Ladies' Home Journal* saluted my achievement, and one of New York's leading literary agents, Julian Bach, took me on as a client.

Now that I had an agent, I was really into the writerly world. Flagged to readers by the *Times* cover photo of a peregrine, I had arrived! Thanks to the *Times* and my colleagues there who had seen merit in the piece, I was launched. Nothing that I have written in the forty-five-plus years since then has created such a wonderful stir!

More important, my piece was *news*: DDT depredation of birds already was well known. Rachel Carson had publicized it widely in her *Silent Spring*, published several years earlier. But Carson had documented DDT's direct lethality, its immediate toxic effect, in which suburban lawns were carpeted with dead and dying song birds that had ingested it. Carson did not consider the more subtle, but equally deadly effect of DDT on raptors, which continued to survive, while their toxin-laced eggshells led to invisible reproductive failure.

This new threat was news to most Americans. It helped galvanize biologists' efforts to study and document the damage; and, with growing help from the federal government, they began to search for ways to stop it. (DDT was banned from most uses in the U.S. in 1972 . Since then, too, there have been dozens, perhaps hundreds of news reports on these efforts to counter DDT deaths and restore endangered North American peregrines and other threatened raptors.)

PEREGRINES WERE AN EXAMPLE of what I later came to call my "weenie theory" of reporting! You bite down on the bread and are taken aback to discover that there is a hot dog — something tasty! — inside. In other words, it is the surprise that makes the story, and without a surprise — a weenie — there is no drama to write about. With it, there is. These are the stories I have sought to write.

Falconers, in most bird watchers' eyes, were the bad guys. They obtained their falcons and other hawks by taking them from inside or near their natal nests. Certainly very many peregrines and other raptors had left the wild in this way. But — and here was the weenie — when these birds fell into trouble from DDT, it was precisely the falconers, Tom Cade and his associates, who possessed the skills and interest to breed them in cages for later release to the wild — something that in fact had never before been done.

This was *news*: the first public revelation that scientists were at work trying to reverse the fate of these doomed birds.

15

PAUL SPITZER

Tom Cade had a Cornell graduate student, Paul Spitzer, who tried a different tack to save a threatened bird population. The nation's fish eagles, *ospreys* — huge chocolate-and-white birds that breed in large stick nests built atop trees or on manmade poles along the edges of marshes and streams — also were in trouble from DDT. The ospreys picked up their toxic loads of pesticide from the fish that are their constant diet. Their eggshells were breaking, and their numbers were declining throughout the country. But they were not as far gone as the peregrines, and there was this difference: Ospreys in some areas were doing better than those in others.

Specifically, the ospreys in New England, while continuing to build nests and lay eggs, were producing next to no young birds. But farther south, around Chesapeake Bay, there was less toxic pollution, and the ospreys were reproducing at a near normal rate. What would happen, Cade and Paul Spitzer wondered, if you took newly laid eggs from osprey nests on the Chesapeake, carried them north, and put them in osprey nests there, after first removing their own doomed eggs? Audubon disliked the idea, but the Fish and Wildlife Service, a part of the Interior Department, was willing to take a chance.

So Spitzer drove to Maryland and collected osprey eggs from nests there. (Fortunately, ospreys that lose their eggs will mate and lay again, a trait called *double-clutching*. So there was little loss to the Chesapeake colony.) So again, contrary to Joseph Hickey and the conservation establishment, there were things that *could* be done to rescue a dwindling bird population — a practice that I came to call *clinical ornithology.* Spitzer's method was proven to work, and he continued with it for several years until the ban on DDT re-thickened the Connecticut ospreys' eggshells, and they began to reproduce themselves in a more normal way. I have been delighted to have been their herald!

I continued to write about Paul, who has become a lifelong friend, and Tom Cade and his growing circle of associates as they created methods to assist threatened raptor populations. It is wonderful to note, forty-five years later, that their work has stabilized the East Coast ospreys and brought peregrines back so that they again exist, sparsely, in most of the lower forty-eight states. Indeed, there is a pair of peregrines nesting not far from my home, in Barnet, Vermont. You can see them in breeding season, perched on branches overlooking the Passumpsic River, or flying, rapidly with deep-dipping wings, toward their aerie in the cliffs above.

Spitzer's experiment showed, in the end, that osprey eggs from elsewhere would be accepted and hatched by birds in New England, and that the chicks would be fed and nurtured by their "adoptive" parents until they fledged. They also would return, years later, to breed there, rather than return to their place of conception in Chesapeake Bay — as it had been feared they would.

Following receipt of his doctoral degree from Cornell, Spitzer embarked on a career as a freelance field biologist, studying and writing reports on ospreys as well as loons and other birds. He now lives in Maryland but visits Northern Vermont each summer in pursuit of his research career. It gives me much pleasure to welcome him here each year.

THE YEAR 2018 WAS THE FIFTIETH ANNIVERSARY of Paul's college graduation from Wesleyan University in Middletown, Connecticut. His alma mater paid him a signal honor: Many of his classmates have thrived in establishment careers as businessmen and bankers. Paul has survived — and sometimes thrived — all these years as a freelance biologist, on private grants and public contracts with the Federal Government and wildlife agencies. Wesleyan chose him to deliver a keynote talk on his career as an independent conservation biologist.

When Tom Cade died early in 2019, Paul wrote of his working with him on his doctorate in the 1970s at Cornell: "That decade was the making of me as a humanist and scientist; and I was there's thanks to the sponsorship, protection, and faith of my incomparable mentor Prof. Tom Cade.

"Ithaca is famous for gray, dreary lake-effect weather. Tom's bright countenance, humor, and perennial optimism dispelled that miasma. For we his students and colleagues . . . and for his many benchmark research-and-management projects, that happy faith and confident intellectual clarity were a foundation for our scholarship, research, and personal growth."

16

PROBE

WANTED TO BE FREER IN MY WRITING: I wanted to cover news that was hidden and did not make it into the media, like the fact that there was a way to stop much of the AIDS epidemic — and it was being ignored. And I wanted to express my opinion — my point of view — in my reports.

The model I aspired to was *I.F. Stone's Newsletter*. This was an incisive four-pager that Stone, a well-known journalist, published every fortnight in Washington, D.C. His beat was politics and government. Mine would be science and medicine and their interaction with government and popular beliefs.

I named my publication *PROBE*, to indicate that I was dissecting news, much as a pathologist uses a probe to dissect tissue at his lab bench.

In a pilot issue dated April 1, 1989, I wrote, "New

Needles Could Stop AIDS." The disease was then running rampant among male homosexuals and IV (intravenous) drug users. I wrote that the "bottleneck" in AIDS transmission among druggies was the *hypodermic syringe*:

A drug addict places the tip of his syringe in the heroin or other drug, and pulls back the plunger to suck the drug into the barrel of the syringe. Then he (or she) sticks the needle into a blood vessel in his arm or other body part. He pushes the plunger down, forcing the drug into his body. Then — and this is the key moment — he draws the plunger back, sucking his blood back into the barrel of the syringe. He does this to loosen and pick up any bits of drug that may have adhered to the barrel's wall. Then he pushes the plunger down a second time, so that the blood and any drug it has picked up squirt into his body. If there are AIDS virus particles in his blood, some of them will have stuck to the inside of the barrel. Then, if a second addict picks up the syringe and repeats the process, some of this virus will be squirted into his circulation. Thus he can become infected.

AIDS spread among drug-users — and thousands, and soon tens of thousands of them were infected. Most died.

Epidemiologists, I wrote, seek the weakest link in this

chain of transmission, which, if pinched, would halt the virus's spread. A *self-destruct needle* that could be used only once would block it.

"Unfortunately," I wrote, "this needle has yet to be invented." But, I quickly added: "With government encouragement — and money — a self-destruct (SD) needle could be quickly developed."

This possibility of course had already struck scientists, inventors, and tinkerers across the country; a number of designs that worked in principle had been built. The obvious next step: Develop and test a prototype that could be manufactured cheaply, and test it in the drug-using community. But this was where progress stopped.

The best-qualified entity to move the matter forward was the major U.S. supplier of hypodermic syringes, the Becton-Dikinson company. An executive there told me that B-D in fact was working to develop a non-reusable needle. But it appears that the company never developed and tested such a device. The federal government, in the person of the Surgeon General, Dr. C. Everett Koop, did not return my phone calls requesting comment. The fed took little, if any, visible initiative in this direction.

I continued to call attention to the lethal anomalies in medical and governmental responses to the AIDS crisis. Irrational considerations governed these responses — and AIDS victims continued to die as the result.

My understanding of public health was that in a crisis,

Medicine and government are equal-opportunity saviors. But with AIDS, because of the stigma of drug use and homosexuality, the establishment reneged on these commitments. This was maddening. Here was a major epidemic threat, and the responsible forces and voices in the country (and in the world) were ducking the life and death challenges!

PROBE said this and continued saying it. I kept on advocating rational methods to curb the epidemic, particularly self-destruct needles. To this end *PROBE* co-sponsored a scientific development conference at the New York University Medical Center. But we never were able to spur business, science, or government to seriously pursue this option.

I was by no means the only person who saw the lifesaving possibility of SD needles. A few years later I reported in *PROBE* (August 1995) that, by 1991, the U.S. Patent and Trademark Office had issued or had pending more than a hundred patents for such a device. Some eighty new ones were registered between July 1994 and July 1995. In New York City, two high school juniors won $15,000 college scholarships for an SD needle that they claimed they had designed. But no agency had adopted this approach and turned it into a public health campaign. Thousands of lives were lost to AIDS as the result.

These *PROBE* banner headlines indicate the stories I published:

- "Is American Science Corrupt?" [11/91]

- "Gun Bans May Not Stop Mayhem" [2/92]
- "Media's Pro-Tobacco Bias Proven" [3/92]
- "Vitamin Bs [as in bullshit] Boosts Sales" [5/92]
- "Science Skunked in Schools By Animal Rights Agitprop" [10/92]
- "Was *New England Journal* Snookered? Media Blitz for Mind/Body Malarkey" [3/93]
- "Malthus Revisited: Should Starving Children Be Fed?" [5/93]
- "Sidestream Cigarette Smoke Called a Major Killer — Is It?" [7/95]
- "With Need Unclear, Risks Muted, Science Police Are Forging Ahead" [8/93]
- "The Lady or the Tiger: DNA Tests Pose Deadly Dilemma" [2/94]
- "Major Broadsheets Bow to Hysteria In Coverage of Breast Cancer Fraud" [4/94]
- "Public Is Scientifically Illiterate, Federally-Funded Study Shows" [9/94]
- "Supreme Court Will Not Allow Brainless Baby Girl To Die" [10/94]
- "Fed's Investigator Testifies: Major Scien-

tific Misconduct Cases Were 'Biased'
Against the Defendants" [12/94]

MY COLLEAGUE AND FRIEND TED KLEIN tipped me on an incredible story, an exclusive. What, Ted asked me, does a pro-life woman do when she discover that she is pregnant, and does not want to be? The answer, he said, is simple. She has an abortion.

She has an abortion!

How did he know?

Ted told me there was an abortion clinic in St. Louis whose patients were asked questions like, *What were your feelings about abortion before you faced an unwanted pregnancy? Why did you come here for an abortion? Have your feelings about it changed, and if so, how? Etc.* Wishing to learn more about these women's answers, I flew to St. Louis to visit the Reproductive Health Services (RHS) clinic. It appears to have been the *only* abortion clinic whose clients were questioned in this way, with their answers recorded. The women said, "Abortion is murder," or "It is taking a human life."

Why then were they having it?

> "I got three children. The father is married. I believe in my heart it was the right thing to do."
>
> "Not wanting this baby because it wasn't my husband's."

"Financial — I live all alone."

"Unmarried, Catholic, [family] would be surprised, embarrassed, hurt."

"I was leaving in a few days to be a freshman at college . . . . I would have lost all respect and support of my parents, because they expect me to become as highly educated as they were. [They] would *not* have financially supported me and my child."

"I am divorced with . . . two children that I can barely provide for."

"My boy friend abandoned me . . . ."

When, finally, these conflicted, mostly young women came to RHS for their procedures, many said, however, that they were *different* from the other women waiting alongside them. (Abortion providers had come to the conclusion that *sisterhood* was the most calming possible ambience in their waiting areas. So they contrived to keep them filled with patients waiting their turns.)

The pro-life women disliked these encounters. They told attendants they were unlike "the others" — they were *different*, good girls — and so should wait separately from the rest.

The topper, described by a doctor from a different clinic, involved an affluent white woman who brought her black maid for an abortion, which the white woman paid for. "While the maid was in a counseling session," the doctor recalled, "a commotion was heard outside in the waiting room. . . . The patient's employer was there handing out *anti-abortion leaflets* to the women waiting for their abortions!"

What did pro-life women do when their abortions were done? Some returned to *anti*-abortion picket lines!

Hypocrisy? Yes, hypocrisy in spades — not only at RHS, but at a half dozen or so other abortion clinics across the country whose administrators I interviewed for *PROBE*. This report was an exclusive. This behavior, as I wrote, has never been carefully reported, or documented in the public prints.

PROBE SEEMED TO BE what I was cut out to do. It suited me perfectly. But there was a fatal flaw.

With the few subscriptions that I had managed to sell, I was essentially paying for *PROBE* out-of-pocket. It also was exhausting work. With no prospects for help from any quarter, I very reluctantly stopped. I shut *PROBE* down.

My great failure was my inability to attract anyone else — specifically, *anyone* with money . . . or a publishing company that would integrate *PROBE* into a magazine or other journalistic vehicle. No one else was doing what I was. But I had not found any publisher who saw the value of an independent voice in the science and "government" policy area in which I was working.

17

DRUG GUIDE

I HAD PRODUCED THIRTY ISSUES, running some 250 pages, over the course of several years. I was exhausted. So I refunded some subscriptions and called it quits. I was very sorry to have had to do so.

We now had our two boys in private school (Ethical Culture), and my wife Veva suggested that I find a more lucrative project.

After a while, one came to hand. I read, in a tiny squib in the *Chicago Tribune*, that the Food and Drug Administration had released part of a new and ongoing scientific and medical review of nonprescription drugs, which are also called *over-the-counter* (OTC) drugs. These are the very many simple remedies — pain killers, sun tan creams, itch relievers — that people can buy without a doctor's prescription. Virtually everyone uses them. Until now, however, there had been no standard guide for consumers to use in order to know which of these products were effective and safe — did what they were advertised to do — and which, on the other hand, were ineffective and might prove to be dangerous. Snake oil, as it were. The FDA was rectifying this situation by convening panels of medical experts to analyze, *not* the products themselves, of which there were thousands, but rather their medically active ingredients, of which there were relatively few, and the combinations of these ingredients and the dosages (amounts) of each found in OTC products such as Anacin and Life Bouy soap. This review process was extremely thorough. Drug companies, or the FDA itself, identified the ingredients in each product; then the FDA assigned each of them to an appropriate panel of experts. Each panel, with a half dozen or so experts, focused on one type of ingredient: pain reliever, dandruff shampoo, digestive aids, etc. They read the scientific and medical literature on each ingredient and rated each one as: Safe and Effective, Safe but Not Effective, Unsafe but Effective, or Not Safe nor Effective. Then, with the help of FDA staffers, the experts wrote a *monograph*, an essay, on each ingredient. Some of these reports ran over a hundred pages of small type in the *Federal Register*, where they were published.

The drug makers who used each ingredient in their products, and anyone else who wished to for that matter, then answered the experts, accepting their judgments or challenging them, saying that the experts had misinterpreted the published scientific literature or were downplaying an ingredient that consumers, by their long use of drug products that contained it, had demonstrated to be Safe and Effective. The experts reviewed these comments, and a second draft, incorporating the drug makers' critiques and the experts' responses, was prepared by FDA and published in the *Federal Register*. One more cycle of proposed label language for each ingredient and its evaluation by the experts followed. Then FDA published a final monograph. Ingredients that were judged Safe and Effective (S&E) could remain on market, in approved dosages. All others were banned — removed from products marketed in interstate commerce.

This was an exemplary project for FDA. The problem was that each review took a long time: years and years from start to finish. It was almost an endless project.

My effort was to summarize the experts' findings in a useful way so that consumers could use them when purchasing OTC products for themselves and their families. I realized that the experts' first assessments provided a benchmark with which to judge each ingredient and, therefore, the OTC products that contained them. These assessments might change as the review progressed, and some did, but odds were that most of the experts' initial judgments would be upheld at the end. In other words, while the OTC Review was work in progress, it could be used to evaluate the safety and efficacy of the millions of products already sold in drug and convenience stores.

That gave me an idea: Why not use the OTC Review to write a manual on the ingredients and products that contained them, as a consumers' guidebook? It appeared that no one else had come up with this idea, or if they had, they had not followed through.

This quickly turned into a massive project. Each report went through three iterations. So in the end, writing this guide book, which ran quite long, took me several unexciting years to write. It was a far cry from peregrine falcons. (A second edition, a few years later, was called *Zimmerman's Complete Guide to Nonprescription Drugs*)

My book did not do as well. For one thing, the publisher, Visible Ink Press, was not into media publicity and other efforts to create sales. It was a secondary company, located in Detroit, that marketed its books via catalogues, mailing lists, and so on. It did not create any excitement for my book. They sold a few copies — some tens of thousands, but not enough to justify the time and enormous amount of work that the project entailed.

At the end, while my *Guide* was in press, a Ralph Nader-linked organization produced a rip-off version. Whether they were aware of my work or came up with the idea on their own, I don't know. They produced a book, which was sold in bookstores, that covered some, but no means all, of the material I was using. It was incomplete and full of errors. But with the publicity that it garnered as the product of a consumer-oriented health organization, it was reported and featured in the media. So it sold, and even made at least one best-seller list.

18

SANKOFA

M Y CHOICE OF A SUBJECT for my next book turned out, after five or six years of labor, to be a bust, from the points of view of impact, income, and professional recognition. In retrospect, I might better have consulted the guidebook *Literary Marketplace* to choose a popular subject. I sought a topic that was hotter — more *engagé* — than Alka Seltzer and asprin: science, say, and crime. Instead, I wanted to solve a problem myself, not simply describe others' successes.

So, I followed my own instinct, and I chose to write about a cemetery — a three-hundred-year-old cemetery in the heart of Manhattan.

This cemetery had been abandoned and covered over in the early eighteenth century. But the 1990s, it was being excavated and brought back into the light.

This was a slave cemetery. It contained the remains of hundreds of black people who had been brought to New York in bondage during Dutch Colonial rule and the earliest decades of rule by the English, who supplanted them. The cemetery had been opened in about 1640 and closed in about 1700, after which Lower Manhattan was built atop it. The site is near Chinatown, and the "dig" was watched daily by New Yorkers as they went about their business.

The excavation created much public interest. The *African Burial Ground*, as it came to be called, was quickly thrust into the front-page news of the day. It demonstrated, dramatically, that slavery was not only a Southern affair. It had afflicted the North, too. The cemetery also raised this question for some black activists: Did these moldering bones provide any evidence, any sign, of these men and womens' African roots? It was a rhetorical question, not a scientific one: There was ample evidence that these were African people.

Once the effort to dig them up was well under way, the black leader of the project, an anthropologist named Michael Blakey, Ph.D., misidentified some faded markings on a fragile coffin lid as tribal symbols from Africa. But, they later were shown to be a date, 1745 — presumably the year of the interred person's burial.

I was initially drawn, as many New Yorkers were, to the heartbreaking stories of these coerced and violated early Americans. But as time went by, I became more and more interested in the recovery work and the project's ongoing direction, which in the end cost *millions of tax payer dollars*. I tried, through the public relations people on the project, to interview Michael Blakey. But he declined to see me — the first scientist in my career to rebuff my request to talk about his work.

Blakey's behavior eventually persuaded me that *he*, not the cemetery, was the story worth pursuing, if for no other reason than that my colleagues, who were uncritically retailing his pronouncements to the public, were not doing so. The clues to Blakey's *folie* were pretty apparent. Why was I the only one to see them?

One reason was that I was looking for just that sort of story. Science writers were — and I think many still are — trapped in an unreal world of *progress*, like the NASA space program. They rarely come up against the crime and punishment that make-up a large part of the daily media report. They are immunized from the real world by science.

I was looking for a science story that dealt with this reality. Michael Blakey seemed to me to be just such a story — and one that was further complicated by the fact that he was black. The media *geist* at the time was to applaud *all* Roots discoverers, not question their probity.

(I had another, less professional reason for pursuing the study of an apparently phony black Roots man: My brother-in-law, Henry Hampton, who was black, had emerged as a leading media person through his effort —

which was highly successful — to depict the civil rights story in his award winning TV series *Eyes on the Prize*. He had pre-empted my self-appointed role as *the* family journalist. I was jealous!)

My resolve was further stimulated when I was invited by Nobel Prize winner David Baltimore to a conference on black scientists' work. There, a young black researcher who had briefly worked with Blakey revealed that the African Burial Ground research was in disarray. Blakey was screwing up a highly visible and quite costly research project.

This was of course an inherently difficult self-assignment: Criticizing Blakey in print would open me to legal risk. I had to work carefully to avoid it: back up all my statements with documents and/or two independent sources, for example. I had to give Blakey an opportunity to challenge my accusations. I tried to set up a meeting with him. He didn't answer my phone calls or letters. So I dealt with his associate. She promised to convey my request for a meeting to him. Still he did not answer.

He was ducking me. How could I prove it? Fortunately, he had "returned to sender" — me — one of my letters requesting an interview. Here was the proof I sought that I had tried to contact him to no avail. I rented a safe deposit box and put the returned letter in it. I believe it is still there!

Fortunately, too, Blakey's Burial Project's problems had, by then, begun to be remarked upon by others, whom I now could quote.

On February 5, 2001, the tabloid *New York Daily News* published a story with this front page banner head-line: "21 Million Plan Mired in Woe — Researchers, Feds Wrangle over ABG" [African Burial Ground]. This reporter wrote, "[t]he project held great scientific potential and tre-mendous cultural value. Today it is mired in racial mistrust, funding feuds, and bickering. . . ." Blakey is quoted as blaming racism. "'What [the Fed] has demonstrated,'" he said, "'is that it still wants black people to work for free!'"

Subsequently, Blakey bad-mouthed the university that was administering his federal grants. He was fired from the burial ground project.

He had by then moved four hundred sets of excavated remains to his lab at Howard University in Washington, D.C. He had hired a staff, most of whom were black, to work on the project. The one exception was the *osteologist*, the bone specialist, who was charged with studying the re-mains. She was a southern white woman from Alabama, Mary Cassandra Hill, M.A. She had worked at the autopsy table twelve to fifteen hours a day to analyze each set of re-mains — work that won high marks from her osteologic colleagues. But just as she was about to finish, Blakey fired her and denied her scientific credit for what she had done. He thereby wrecked her scientific career.

The following year, his first report unfinished, Blakey was quoted in the *Washington Post* (August 27, 2002) as saying "There is a gun to our heads . . . what the [fed] is insisting on is for us to fail . . . I think racism plays a special part as well as arrogance. The [fed] has demonstrated from the beginning a pattern of disrespect and disregard for the expertise of black people."

The government had by then spent or committed $21 million for the project. But Blakey said, scoffingly, "We did not need what is often called in black college circles, 'a colored grant'."

Needless to say, this outburst, and the poor research work behind it, blew up the project, and ended Blakey's control of it.

So I had my story. But getting it published was another matter. I could not find a publisher who wanted it as "*SANKOFA? How Racism and Sexism Skewed New York's Epochal Black Research Project.*" So I self-published it.

My next job was to publicize it by placing magazine articles that summarized my findings in major magazines. Here I was blown away! At the *New York Times*, the obvious place, neither the daily paper nor the magazine wanted it. So I turned to the main science mags. Neither *Nature* nor *Science* was interested either. If some scientific or governmental agency had leveled charges against Blakey, they probably would have published them. But I was *only* a freelance writer, with no organization at my back. Blakey was a   scientist. I could be — and I was — ignored.

Maybe I could get other print or media coverage. I

hired a public relations woman: $10,000 for three months. *She* failed to get me a single line of type!

Self-publishing a book, as I did, is a desperate last-ditch effort to reach readers. Self-publishing a counterintuitive expose of a black activist scientist, I now know, was an invitation to failure. Without the distinction and promotional resources of a commercial publishing company, the chances for success were nil.

If, say, the *New York Times* had published my story, chances are that the Sankofa nonsense would have been removed from the burial site, so that it reflected the historical truth about it that a hundred million dollars worth of research had uncovered. If *Science* or *Nature* had published my findings in any form, the pseudo-science by Michael Blakey might have been expunged from the scientific record. None of this has happened. I sold very few copies

Clearly, a lone journalist such as myself is going to have a hard time reporting the truth about a situation where there is no support from an established media source.

(My book can be purchased from Amazon for $16.00.)

19

FAMILY DISCORD

I HAVE BEEN SO EAGER TO SETTLE SCORES with my mother in these pages that I have given short shrift to an underlying sad problem: Our family was in discord, and eventually disintegrated.

This did not have much to do with me. It was more about an irrevocable conflict between my father and my mother. It was a clash of personalities. Sex had a whole lot to do with it.

Zim, unlike my mother, was a nice person — a nice man. And a proper one.

He did not swear or blow farts. He came to the dinner table wearing his suit and tie. As I remember him, he was kind to people, and as the Great Surgeon, he took responsibility, and was helpful to his mother and her large family. (He was the second, and most academically advanced, of her eight children.) When I was young, he seemed at peace with the world. Later, less so.

One conflict I noticed early on: Zim was a whittler. He carved soap animals for me, and bit by bit he started carving wood. He carved women, some fully nude, but none in bad taste. He advanced his whittling tools from ordinary chunks of wood and a pocket knife to ever harder tropical woods like monkey pod, and Xacto knives. He liked, late in the day, to sit in the back yard or on the back porch and whittle. One result: wood chips on the grass and sidewalk.

My mother grew irritated by Zim's "mess." She insisted he put down a catch cloth and sweep up after himself. This struck me as odd at the time. (I was in my early teens.) He was doing something artistic; he showed his pieces at art shows, and won prizes for them.

The shavings were clean and seemed to me to be quite harmless. But my mother was insistent. She scolded him till he cleaned the shavings and chips.

But it was galling. He was being attacked for having minor fun in the backyard of the house *he* had bought with his earnings. How could she tell him what to do? She did!

Perhaps my mother disliked his subject matter — nude women! Perhaps he chose them to irritate her! I'll never know. But her tidy sense of order clearly was mobilized against him!

Then, as I only learned much later, why hadn't he told my mother that my sister, Judy, was threatened by a birth defect, *patent ductus arteriosus*. And, once he did, why did she go to the mat with him, insisting that he was wrong about it? She had no medical training. He did. She must have been furiously angry to challenge him.

World War II enhanced their conflict. Zim was old enough that he did not have to serve, and Sally urged him to stay home. With the younger doctors off to war, she said, Zim should stay and cash in on their absence. But he insisted he was going. He signed up with the U.S. Navy, and was given an appointment as a Lieutenant Junior Grade (JG).

I remember him going away, partly because, at his farewell party, I ate all the fruit from the punch bowl. I became quite drunk. I went to the second floor, where the guests' coats were piled in a bedroom. I threw them down the front stairs, then parked myself on the dining room floor — and fell asleep.

Zim went ahead to Seattle, where he was assigned to a naval hospital. I was ill — I don't remember with what — and I protested vehemently when Zim's elder brother Harry insisted on wheeling me in a buggy from the streetside of the station to our train, the Empire Builder, for the dramatically beautiful, forty-five-plus-hour ride to the Pacific Coast.

Zim wound up after two years at a rear hospital on Guam, where men who had been injured at the front were stabilized for their long journey home. It was light duty, and there was time for Zim to play. Judging by a few photos I saw later of bare breasts and native women with grass skirts, he played around a lot. I hope now, decades later, that he had fun!

My mother, sister, and I went home in 1944. He followed us, a year later, after the Japanese surrender. No reconciliation resulted.

Zim was not kind to my mother. During the war, she had started an art gallery at our temple to serve refugee artists from Europe. After the war she wanted to go commercial with it. Zim refused to let her: Doctors' wives do *not* work for money!

20

END OF THE ZIM'S

A T THIS POINT, ZIM MADE a new friend, a young European woman, a professional historian, Ilza Veith, Ph.D. She shared his interest in medical history and was already renowned for having translated the fundamental medical text, *The Yellow Emperor's Classic of Internal Medicine*, from Chinese to English. She was interested in medically historical methods like acupuncture (she had me shop for acupuncture needles in Paris, where I then was studying.)

Ilza and Zim wrote a book together; they traveled together. But neither of them divorced their spouses, which no doubt infuriated Sally. Then, Ilza was given an appointment at Stanford University and moved to California. Very shortly, she suffered a debilitating stroke and lived there with her husband Hans. She died in 2013.

Sally retaliated. She evicted Zim from their bed and the master bedroom. She moved him to a small space by the back elevator of the building in which they were living. She occupied the master bedroom by herself. Their estrangement was the final step in the demise of the Zimmerman family.

Through it all, the one bond that lasted and grew was between Zim and my sister Judy. They loved each other!

I was gone from Chicago during Zim's last act, and I don't know what, if any, role I played in it. My impression is that it unfolded with little reference to me.

Judy and I were Zim's heirs. My mother told me she had kept track of every check he had written to help me pay for my psychoanalysis. She *subtracted* that amount, about five thousand dollars, from the inheritance she sent me. She chastised me for hanging out with the University of Chicago communists, for going into psychoanalysis, and for much of the rest of my life.

She started to tell me, "If, instead, you had done what I thought you should do, then —"

I hung up.

Now, I'm sorry I did; it would have been interesting to learn what kind of a horrid life she had in mind for me!

21

SUE

SHERRY AND JUDY GORBACH, WHO HAD introduced me to my first wife, Veva, did it again! The scene was Brandeis, where we had gathered for class reunions in June 2011.

As I walked out of one event, I saw the Gorbachs chatting with a woman whom I did not immediately recognize. The Gs introduced me: Susan (Geller) Gold, a classmate from long ago. She was talking to them about a book she had just written, *The Eyes Are The Same*, and she handed me a copy.

I remembered that she had been born in the Ukraine and had spent the Nazi occupation there, hidden with her parents in a *bunker* — a room-sized space dug under a farmer's barn. The book Sue handed me, which was published by Full Court Press, described her time in the dark with Nazi boots above. She had been seven years old when she went underground. The family hid there for two years, until the Russians liberated the area in the spring of 1944, and it was safe to come out. They were among the fortunate few survivors. Millions of Jews from their area had been sent to death camps.

When the Nazis entered Zolochiv, Sue's home town in 1940, some 9,000 Jews lived there, meaning that there were about 3,000 children. When the Red Army liberated the area in 1944, seven children were left alive. Sue was one, along with her two cousins, and three friends. A seventh survivor was a boy named Roald Hoffman.

In 1981, the Nobel Prize for research chemistry was awarded to Roald Hoffman.

Two of Sue's family did not survive — her little brother, Janek (Jacob), could not keep quiet in the bunker. To prevent him from alerting the Nazis to the family's presence, Sue's grandmother left the bunker with Janek. They were never seen again. The Gellers learned later that grandmother and Janek had been caught and been killed at Bergen-Belsen.

After the war, the Gellers made their way west through Europe, where they entered a displaced persons (D.P.) camp near Munich. A year later, a relative in the U.S. found their names on a D.P. list and arranged for them to come to America, in fact to Brooklyn, where they were set up to run a small food store.

Susan had been taught to read and write and also to speak Russian by her father, and now learned English. She had no elementary schooling. Her father taught her the alphabet with newspaper headlines.

One day, when Sue was a high school senior, a friend directed a Brandeis University recruitment dean to interview her. He had been a U.S. Army liberator of Auschwitz. The Dean was smitten by Susan! He recruited her at once — and the following autumn, 1952, she entered Brandeis, where she thrived. She graduated with a Bachelor's degree in 1956.

At the time, I thought she was sexually provocative. She thought I was "cute" — a girls' word meaning "of erotic interest." She was impressed by my Chicago origins, my social leadership, and my sure-sounding bantering about campus life and political issues — but she disliked my naive leftist outlook.

We rarely spoke to each other, never dated, and both graduated as virgins, me because of my reticence, she because her mother insisted that she save herself to marry a doctor — which she did.

Sue and I never saw each other in the half century between graduation and the reunion with the Gorbachs. I knew that she had worked in Russia: She had been hired by AIG and other large multinational companies in New York because of her facility with the Russian language. I had thought she must be in the CIA. But, she told me, she had tried but had been rejected because of her Polish and Russian background.

We came to know each other surprisingly quickly. Each of us felt compelled to explain where we had been psychosexually in the interim.

Her husband's name was Elliot Gold. He was a brash, money-hungry Jewish Bostonian, who was an undergraduate student at Harvard. They had been wed in high style. She'd joined him in the peripatetic life that doctors in training then were forced into by the requirement that they spend time in military service. The Golds came to ground in New York City. They started a family there: a girl, Liza, then two boys, Jonathan and Peter.

Sue had continued her studies after Brandeis. She joined the Russian Institute at Columbia University, studying the country's history, and improving her language skills. She got a job teaching Russian at the Bronx High School of Science.

Elliot was not a great lover, Susan allowed. He rarely captured her gaze to look at her eye to eye. He had many male friends, with whom he spent much time. Over the years, in fact, Susan came to realize that these were homosexual relationships, which he maintained, to her bewilderment.

The girl, Liza, grew up and, with some reluctance, she followed her dad and went to medical school, at New York University. There, by happenstance, she met my wife, Veva, who was a dean at the school. Liza's ambivalences had gotten her into academic difficulties, and she was often sent to see the dean. Veva had had similar ambivalences during her medical training, and had come close to failing her senior year. So she knew the drill, and helped Liza get through to her M.D.

Meanwhile, Sue's younger son, Peter, at age twelve, had suddenly become very ill. He had suffered an aneurysm and died of a congenital bleed in the brain. It was between Christmas and New Year's 1988. Sue has never recovered from his death. She pines for him often these many years later.

By the 1980s the Golds were living a high-style suburban life and also had a penthouse in the city. But Elliot's health was not good. He had flu-like episodes. And a ministroke. Liza observed his symptoms and made a diagnosis. Mom. she said, I think dad has AIDS!

Elliot knew what was the matter. He told Sue, from a hospital bed, "I know who gave it to me." Overwhelmed by his betrayal, Susan stood up, walked out of the hospital, and sued Elliot for divorce. After several chaotic years, Elliot died of AIDS in 1995.

About this time, Russian Premier Mikhail Gorbachev opened his country to Western businesses. There was a rush to open offices in Moscow. The problem was that few Americans spoke the language well enough to staff them. Sue did, and so was quickly hired. She commuted to Russia for more than twenty years. She set up an apartment there, where she lived for three years, until Boris Yeltsin ended perestroika and American businesses pulled out.

Sue returned to New Jersey — which is where she lived when we met again in 2011. She had just written and published the biographical account of her time in the bunker during the Nazi occupation. In it, she describes her long life in terror from a child's point of view — which has led some commentators to call her "the American Anne Frank" for writing about the Holocaust from that chilling child's perspective. Few kids live in mortal fear when they are six or seven years old. She had.

Sue and I bonded quickly. "We both have had dreadful lives!" she explained. And, she and I believe, we are two people who have been very fortunate to have found each other at the end.

I asked myself, should I abandon my protective reticence to come on to her? A voice within me, a voice I never had heard before or since, said, "I knew her before!"

I'm not sure why I heard that. But I did as it suggested. First, I invited her to spend a weekend with me in my Vermont house. I showed her to a ground-floor bedroom and told her I would sleep on the second floor, and that she was welcome to join me. She didn't.

Soon, we went on a vacation together in Spain. In a hotel room there, we found that we could talk freely about our love lives — which I had never before done with a date

— and practice sex together in a way that for me was not anxiety provoking because Sue didn't admonish me to "get it up, or leave!"

Part of the reason for her encouraging attitude was the fact that I quickly learned to pleasure her and bring her to orgasm with my finger tips and tongue.

I could induce her to come, loudly and long. My own, more masturbatory, orgasms were far weaker but were adequate. Regrettably, there was little reciprocity. She could not get me to come, either because of her lack of skill or my reticence (or both), and my lack of erotic sites for her to stimulate. But when I masturbated she would join by kissing me and messing with my face — and then I would come.

It angered me the way she helped me, usually briefly, when I was stimulating her. I felt I was in competition with her — and losing. Later on, she helped me realize that I was bound by the way I had masturbated through the years; I could not reassign my erogenous zones or what I required to come to climax. It was, alas, too late for that.

Lately, I've run out of juice. So it's less a duet now, and more her show. Still, we have had, and continue to have, erotic lives, now into our mid-eighties — something that is rarely discussed in magazine sex columns. It doesn't make up for the decades of suffering we experienced in our lives; nevertheless, it is a balm in old age!

More prosaically, we've found that we get along extremely well. We rarely fight. Our reactions to events are quite similar, albeit she chides me as a left liberal, "a communist," which of course is not true.

I had previously paid little attention to my family's Eastern European origins, but Sue points out that our ancestors come from similar backgrounds. Hers were from Ukraine, while mine were from Lithuania, originally Poland. So I am a Polish–Russian–Ukrainian Jew.

Initially, my fear was that she would kill me, figuratively speaking, by, say, angrily walking out on me. But that has never happened! She has been kind to me. I have been as kind as I know how with her. In five years, we have had disagreements but few angry arguments (except when I am commenting on her driving, or she is giving me directions when I am). Because of the time that she spent underground, with more than a year in D.P. camps, Sue has virtually no linear sense of direction. She cannot locate herself on a grid, which makes driving difficult. She goes where she's been, and when she gets off the path, she quickly becomes lost, and stops passersby to ask for directions — which I dislike her doing.

Susan does not chide me. I've grown slow — "Slow Joe crow!" I tell her — and she does not object! "You're not in a rush now," she will say. "You've done your thing and you're entitled to go slow now!"

I am grateful!

Shockingly, this benign familial feeling faded away in

the winter of 2017–18. Susan very often was angry with me. She seemed insulting and mean. She began calling me names. She made fun of my "clumsiness," my gauche manner of speech, my efforts to be *with it.*

I was abashed by her cruelty. It was a reversal of her earlier kindness and support. I was flabbergasted. I tried to defend myself.

I wondered: Had I stumbled back onto Dorchester Avenue in Chicago? I was again being punished, as my mother would have done. I had no place to escape it.

What could explain this turn of events?

Oddly, the weather and the season had much to do with it. We were in Sheffield at Christmas, where it turned remarkably cold: the temperatures fell to minus 18 degrees Fahrenheit, and the cold night wind blew through the house.

It was a bleak time for us both. Sue became despondent, as she does every early winter. It is the time of the year when Peter died. She could not shake her grief, which peaked at the New Year.

I, meanwhile, had fallen down behind a backing-up taxicab and was almost run over. It took weeks for my bruises to heal.

Just as the season's first blizzard began, we drove out of Vermont headed for Sue's house near Manhattan, in New Jersey. But I missed a turn — and the drive took eight hours instead of six and a half. I went to bed exhausted — and woke up ill. I remained sick from early January till March. I hadn't been that ill since childhood, if then.

My discomfort eventually was traced to *bronchitis*, the rattling in the chest and all. It took an unusually long time to get the doctor to prescribe the cure, tetracycline. It cleared my chest in three days. But I still was weak and chilled. In Florida (Sarasota), I went to the swimming pool every day in the 80–85 degree heat and sat out in the sun wearing a thick green sweater. I couldn't get warm enough.

Then, on our next to last day in Florida, Sue tripped over an open dishwasher in our flat and fractured her knee-cap. We dragged ourselves back to Englewood.

Sue remained frightened and querulous, directing critical imprecations at me. I was simple-minded. I was a slob. I was wasting her time.

She scolded me. Scolded me! As if I were a recalcitrant child! Could she be right, that I was regressing?

I heard — I felt — my mother's voice in each word Sue said. *Was* I a no-good, clumsy oaf? It felt like I was! What could I do to escape the shame? Fortunately, I now had the presence of mind to ask myself: What is Sue doing? It dawned on me that I was not the things Sue was accusing me of — but that *she* was in pain and in a cruel mood, and that most of the things she said were her *meshugas*. I was the prepared victim because of my past.

But now, I would sit stock still — unmoving — absorbing her threats, reassuring myself that her abuses were borne of something inside her, something entirely her own that she was helpless to right.

I noticed that she put on a different and, to me, unfamiliar mien. She was no longer my supportive companion. She was a shrew. I noticed, too, that her mood changes had little to do with what I was saying or doing. It was as if illness and adversity had called up a different and deeply unhappy part of her psyche, without her being aware of these shifts in her being.

She was reliving her time in the bunker, Janek's death, the loss of Peter, and Elliot's betrayal. Despite being aware of these emotions, she could not stop herself from acting them out.

When she was in one of those aggressive states, she was not aware that it was any different from her face of good cheer. She had no inkling, as she moved from one state into another, that she was doing so.

Fortunately, as winter gave way to spring, Sue's anger lessened. When I challenged her, she had a surprising explanation: *She* hurt, and when she hurt, that empowered her — in return — to be as nasty and cruel as she could wish to be. When the world hurt her, she said, she could, and would return blow for blow. Her anger, she explained was aimed at the larger world, not at me.

"But I'm the only one here!" I protested. That seemed to matter little. It wasn't me she was attacking. It was everyone and everything, even though I was the only one about to catch her hell. But her attacks abated, so she must have heard and responded to what I was saying.

"I love you!" she began saying in 2018.

"I love *you*," said I.

IN SUM

ALL IS AS WELL NOW as it has ever been. Nevertheless, I feel that my life has been a failure. Susan disagrees. I have been denied the birth right of masculinity by events that started in Texas, well before my birth. I am enraged but I am stymied.

I do understand that my mother's treatment of me was inadvertent. She didn't know, and probably wouldn't have cared how much damage she created in my life. I understand, but I do not forgive her.

I am proud and pleased with how much I have been able to create, how much I have been able to live and work in this disaster zone — especially my love for Gibby, Veva, Sue and my boys, J.B. and Tobias. I thank them and the many others, like Ralph Norman, who have been kind and supportive. Nevertheless mine has not been a happy life!

—*David Zimmerman*
July 2020